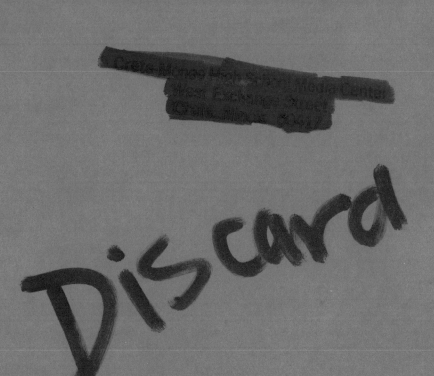

Beyond a Reasonable Doubt

ALSO BY THE AUTHOR

Call the Final Witness:
The People v. Darrell R. Mathes as Seen by the Eleventh Juror

---

BEYOND

A

REASONABLE

DOUBT

Inside the American Jury System

Melvyn Bernard Zerman

Thomas Y. Crowell   New York

For my mother and in memory of my father

Text copyright © 1981 by Melvyn Bernard Zerman
Illustrations copyright © 1981 by John Caldwell
All rights reserved. Printed in the United States of America.
No part of this book may be used or reproduced
in any manner whatsoever without written permission
except in the case of brief quotations embodied
in critical articles and reviews. For information address
Thomas Y. Crowell Junior Books, 10 East 53rd Street,
New York, N. Y. 10022.
Published simultaneously in Canada
by Fitzhenry & Whiteside Limited, Toronto.
Designed by Harriett Barton

Library of Congress Cataloging in Publication Data

Zerman, Melvyn Bernard.
Beyond a reasonable doubt.

SUMMARY: An account of how the American jury
system works and where it sometimes fails.
1. Jury—United States—Juvenile literature.
[1. Jury] I. Caldwell, John, 1946–   II. Title.
KF9680.Z9Z47   347.73'752   80-2451
ISBN 0-690-04094-6   ISBN 0-690-04095-4 (lib. bdg.)

2   3   4   5   6   7   8   9   10
FIRST EDITION

CONTENTS

THE END
OF A
STORY

The Jury Trial

as Drama

It was probably the most famous American murder trial of the last century. In Fall River, Massachusetts, Lizzie Borden stood accused of axing to death her stepmother and her father. The crime was one of extraordinary horror; about thirty blows had been struck by that busy, bloody hatchet, and Lizzie—a thirty-two-year-old unmarried woman of seemingly unblemished moral character, high social standing, and, now, considerable wealth —was a most unlikely defendant. No wonder the case had seized the imagination of people all over the country, had seized it and would not let it go.

In June of 1893, a year of limited national and international unrest, the courthouse of the old whaling port of New Bedford, to which the trial had been moved, became the news center of the United States, attracting such huge, unruly crowds that special fences had to be put up around the building to contain them. From all parts of the land the press sent reporters and artists to cover the event; heavy telegraphic cables snaked from the hall outside the courtroom, across the courthouse lawn, to sending stations set up in neighboring backyards; from there stories of the trial were transmitted to hundreds of newspapers and those millions of readers who waited impatiently for every new and shocking revelation.

Inside the courtroom, the prosecution spent almost seven days presenting its case against Lizzie Borden, the defense a day and a half in maintaining her innocence. Another two days were given to summations by the defense and prosecution and to the Chief Justice's charge to the jury. Before retiring to begin their deliberations, the jurors heard this concluding statement from the judge. While phrased in the language of yesterday and sounding a theological note not commonly heard in courtrooms today, the declaration of the distinguished justice serves here to explain what this book is all about:

> And entering upon your deliberation with no pride of opinion, with impartial and thoughtful minds, seeking only for the truth, you will lift this case above the range of passion and excited feeling, into the clear atmosphere of reason and law. If you shall be able to do this, we can hope that, in some high sense, this trial may be adopted into the order of Providence and may express in its results somewhat of that justice with which God governs the world.

The judge had thus affirmed an ancient and noble ideal. We will never know whether the jurors—twelve middle-aged and elderly farmers—paid much attention to his words or bothered to ponder their meaning. We do know they were quite eager to start their deliberations and in a rush to reach their verdict. Most people in the courtroom, the overwhelming majority of them sympathetic to Lizzie (her father had been both wealthy and miserly, a combination of qualities that made him one of the most unpopular men in Fall River), expected the jury to be out for a long time. The prosecutor's summation had exhaustively reviewed every piece of evidence pointing to the defendant's guilt. Certain facts, though the state's attorney had recalled them in a cool and unemotional way, were inescapably damning in their implications. To consider them all could easily have required more than a day.

The jury was out for precisely one hour. As the twelve men resumed their seats in the jury box, all eyes were fixed upon them. Surprise at their early return added to the drama of the moment, which mounted as one clerk of the court called out the names of each of the jurors and another then commanded, "Lizzie Andrew Borden, stand up." She was instructed to face the jury. The clerk asked the first of two questions that, in various forms and in many languages, have been asked over and over and over again throughout the western world: "Gentlemen of the jury, have you agreed upon your verdict?"

"We have," the foreman answered.

"Lizzie Andrew Borden, hold up your right hand. Mr. Foreman, look upon the prisoner; prisoner, look upon the foreman. What say you, Mr. Foreman—" But before the clerk could finish the second question—"do you find the prisoner guilty or not guilty?"—the foreman interrupted him.

"Not guilty!" he cried.

The verdict was greeted with a deafening burst of applause and a cheer that, according to one newspaper report, "might have been heard half a mile away." Spectators shouted, wept, and climbed on the courtroom benches, waving hats and handkerchiefs. Strangers shook hands, embraced, kissed. Lizzie Borden put her head down on the rail in front of her and sobbed.

It was, then, a scene of total pandemonium in a place accustomed to only the most solemn of proceedings. It was a spontaneous eruption of feelings that had long been held in check by the decorum demanded by the court. It was, above all, the welcome end of a long story, a story full of eccentric characters, dark secrets, and horrifying violence—a story of ever-rising suspense and tension. Although it is doubtful that in their sixty-minute deliberation the jurors had conscientiously performed the task that the judge, in all his florid eloquence, had charged them with —today, most students of the case are convinced that Lizzie Borden did indeed murder her stepmother and her father— there is no question that these twelve good men played to the hilt their parts in the drama. With the foreman delivering the verdict prematurely, not even allowing all of that second ancient question to be asked, the jurors brought the Lizzie Borden story to a most satisfying, slam-bang finish. Leave it to Providence to know whether justice was done. Although the jury may not have acted as responsibly as it should have, it brought a rich human drama to an end with a flourish and, thereby, helped to perpetuate a legend.

The Cast of Characters

While the Lizzie Borden case was perhaps uniquely melodramatic and notorious, every trial resembles Lizzie's in that every trial tells a story—and usually a fascinating one when it is concerned with the commission of a crime. But a trial is also a story in itself, with a beginning, a middle, and, as we have seen, when the verdict is announced, an end. The characters in the story, whatever their names may be, all have specific roles, and in every criminal trial the roles are the same.

There is, first and above all, the judge, who sits at a desk set on a platform called the bench and therefore looms higher than everyone else, reflecting the significance of his position, which is by far the most responsible in the courtroom. When he enters, everybody stands; when he raps his gavel, everybody falls silent; when he speaks, everybody is supposed to listen.

There is the defendant—or there may be more than one—a person or persons accused of having committed a crime.

There is the defense attorney—and again there may be more than one—a lawyer whose job it is to use every possible legal means to get his or her client, the defendant, acquitted—that is, found not guilty—of the crime that has been charged, or, failing that, to see that the defendant receives the least severe sentence.

There is the prosecuting attorney—and again there may be more than one—a lawyer employed by the state whose job it is to present all the available legal evidence to get the defendant convicted—that is, found guilty—of the crime.

There are, as the trial progresses, various witnesses who are summoned by either the defense or the prosecuting attorney, to tell what they know about the crime of which the defendant is accused, or what they know about the defendant himself, or, perhaps, what they know about each other.

There are several clerks and officers of the court, people who perform such jobs as recording on a special machine everything that is said publicly in the courtroom, putting identifying markings on every piece of evidence that is introduced, and administering to witnesses the oath by which they swear to tell "the truth, the whole truth, and nothing but the truth."

And, finally, there is the jury, usually composed of twelve

people, whose job is to decide upon the guilt or innocence of the accused and, in that way, to see that justice is done. Aside from their being of voting age, as is legally required, the members of a jury usually have very little in common. A jury may be composed only of men or only of women or, more likely, of a combination of both. It may include people of only one race or of different races, of widely varying ages, and of a diversity of occupations as well as the unemployed. Sitting side by side may be the rich and the poor and many of those in between, the poorly educated who never managed to obtain a single diploma and the scholars who over the course of their lives have acquired several. The few facts that apply to most jurors best describe what the twelve people are *not*. They do not have law degrees; they are not employees of the court; they are not related or previously known to each other or to anyone else participating in the trial; and they have very limited experience in courtroom procedure, or, more likely, none at all. Thus, in their educational and occupational backgrounds, they are in no way like the judge or the attorneys or the clerks and officers of the court. But they may be like the witnesses and, of course, the defendant.

The Structure of a Trial

The story in which all these characters play their roles follows a very systematic design. Although there may well be surprises during the course of a trial—unexpected developments, sudden turns of fortune for one side or the other—all the events occur within a framework that is as rigidly structured and as dependent upon rules as a baseball game or a commencement exercise.

The trial procedure begins with the selection of a jury, which may take hours, days, or even weeks. Once the choice of jurors has been made, the trial itself begins. The prosecuting attorney always delivers an opening statement; defense counsel usually does. In turn, they outline to the jury exactly what they hope to demonstrate as the trial unfolds. These preliminary speeches are followed by the taking of testimony from witnesses. The prosecution calls its witnesses first, questions them in what is known as direct examination, and allows each to be cross-examined by the defense. Then the defense summons and interrogates its witnesses, who may, in turn, be cross-examined by the prosecution. During the course of questioning, either side, with the permission of the judge, may introduce evidence—documents, photographs, objects—that relates in some way to the crime or the defendant. When the offering of testimony and evidence—which may be thought of as the middle of the trial—is completed, the end is in sight.

Suspense rises as both sides address the jury in final statements called summations. Here defense and prosecution review the evidence that has been presented, each side emphasizing those points that are in its own best interest. The defense attorney probably contends that his client is innocent of the charges against him. Or, if the defendant has confessed to the crime, his lawyer will argue that the reasons for his act (self-defense or temporary insanity, for example) require a verdict of not guilty. At the very least, the defense will insist that the district attorney has not, in the testimony and evidence put forward, succeeded in proving the defendant guilty beyond a reasonable doubt. The prosecutor argues just the opposite—that the defendant has indeed been proved guilty and this judgment must now be affirmed by the jury.

With the conclusion of the two summations, it is the judge's turn to address the jurors. In his statement, called the charge to the jury, he *may* summarize all the material that defense and prosecution have presented in the courtroom; he will definitely explain the law or laws the defendant is accused of having broken and will instruct the jury as to the exact nature of its responsibility. The twelve people who have sat mutely throughout the trial, listening and trying to understand, no doubt fascinated at times and bored at other times, are now invested with a power greater than that of anyone else in the room—that is, the power to determine the facts of the case and, on that basis, the fate of the accused.

The Search for Truth

So a trial is like a story in a couple of ways; it has a cast of characters and a definite structure, one that builds in suspense as it rises to a climax. But a trial is like a story in yet another way, perhaps the most important of all.

Nearly every story is a story of search. Think about that. If you analyze a movie or television play you have seen, a novel or short story you have read, you will realize that on some level, obvious or not, it probably tells of a character or characters trying to find something. Perhaps it is something quite specific, like a person or a sum of money; perhaps something essential, like a home or a job; perhaps something abstract and often hard to recognize, like love, happiness, freedom, or a meaning for life.

A courtroom trial is like a story in that it, too, always tells of a search. But unlike fiction, here the object of the search is unvaryingly the same. The story of a trial is always the story of a search for truth.

Not all the characters whose roles have been described are necessarily engaged in that search. Certainly the defendant, whether or not he is actually guilty of the crime with which he has been charged, wants but one thing—to get himself acquitted. Acting for him in the pursuit of that end is his attorney.

Now a criminal lawyer may, on occasion, proclaim himself a fighter for truth and justice, and, on occasion, he may be precisely that. Nevertheless, having accepted a case, once he enters the courtroom where it is to be tried, a defense lawyer's principal responsibility—indeed, many would say, his only responsibility —is to his client: to see that the defendant leaves the courtroom in freedom and not in handcuffs; or, failing that, to see that his client receives the lightest punishment possible.

On the opposing side is the prosecutor. He, too, may claim that he is seeking truth and justice but in fact he probably is convinced that he already knows the truth. For him to argue his case effectively, he must believe in the defendant's guilt. (If, indeed, during the course of the trial facts are revealed to him that he finds totally inconsistent with guilt, he has a legal obligation to halt the proceedings against the defendant.) The prosecutor's job then becomes one not of search but of persuasion. He must persuade the jury to accept his truth as *the* truth. Justice demands that the defendant pay for his crime.

What about the others in the courtroom? Without a doubt, the judge and the court officers are all eager to learn the facts of the case. But the judge must also be concerned with fairness, with what the law allows in the way of testimony and evidence. Indeed, in order to make certain that neither side in the contest— and that is exactly what a criminal trial is—gains an unfair advantage, the judge must often narrow the channel through which the facts of the case may flow. For any one of a number of reasons, he may prevent witnesses from offering all the testimony they are prepared to give, or he may rule that certain pieces of evidence are not admissible in the trial. In taking such actions, the judge, on the basis of his knowledge and experience, is exercising his authority to determine how the facts are to be disclosed. He is, in effect, balancing the constitutional and legal rights of the accused against the proper and reasonable requirements of the state. He serves thus as protection for both the defendant and the society that the defendant is accused of having in some way harmed. In playing this crucial role, however, the judge is not evaluating the testimony and evidence to decide what the facts of the case may be. No, that task—the job of determining the truth—belongs only to the jury.

The Unpredictability of Juries

So the moment when a jury announces its verdict furnishes us with both the end of a story and the end of a search. But it is not just the structure and the objective of a trial that makes the moment so dramatic. It is also the likelihood that the verdict will be a surprise.

It is true that in some trials the prosecution or the defense builds a case of such overwhelming strength that the outcome of the contest appears to be a foregone conclusion. You may follow such a trial carefully in the newspaper or perhaps as a spectator in the courtroom; as the proceedings draw to a close, you are absolutely certain of what the jury's verdict will be—and the chances are rather good that you will be right. Since juries are composed of ordinary people, they will probably view and weigh the evidence offered to them much as you and I would, and they will come to the same decision. After all, there are what is known as open-and-shut cases where it seems almost unnecessary to send the jury out to deliberate. The verdict is thoroughly predictable.

Or is it? At a trial some years ago in California, a man was accused of murdering his wife. The prosecution set before the jury a mass of evidence that pointed almost unmistakably to the defendant's guilt. But something was missing: the body of the victim. The woman, the defendant's wife, had never been found.

Of course, the defense attorney centered his case around the absent corpse. Although he cross-examined some of the district attorney's witnesses, he called no witnesses and offered no evidence of his own. He reserved almost all his arguments for his summation, and then he gave the dynamic performance that had been expected of him. He was colorful, he was exciting, he was eloquent, he was imaginative—he was, in a word, a showman. As he came to the end of a speech that in countless clever ways repeated a single idea—since no one had been able to prove that a crime had even been committed, how could his client be judged guilty of committing it?—his voice grew louder, his tone more insistent. "Ladies and gentlemen of the jury, you must find my client innocent for one simple reason:"—his voice dropped —"his wife is still alive. In fact"—and now he was speaking barely above a whisper—"she just walked into the courtroom!"

Needless to say, the effect of this announcement was electrifying. Like machines that had suddenly been switched on, the heads of all the jurors and spectators swiveled to the rear of the courtroom—only to find that not a door had opened and not a soul had entered the chamber. An anticlimax perhaps, but a trick that worked; the attorney had made his point.

In a conversational, but still emphatic tone, he explained that he had indulged in his little game in order to demonstrate the obvious: the jurors clearly suspected that the alleged victim might still be alive. In view of this, he concluded, how could they possibly decide beyond a reasonable doubt that the defendant had murdered his wife?

It was a brilliant ploy. Everyone agreed to that. Even the district attorney and his staff felt it was the decisive moment of the trial. And when, after less than an hour, the jury returned to the courtroom, no one was surprised. Given the circumstances, that was time enough.

CALDWELL

Imagine, then, the response when the jury announced its verdict: they found the defendant guilty of murder. The emotion of the instant when all heads had turned to the rear of the courtroom was pale in comparison to the reaction now—compounded of consternation, amazement, and disbelief. And, of course, as the judge hammered his gavel to restore the courtroom to order and went on to thank the jurors for their services, no one was more dumbfounded than the defense attorney. Unaccustomed to losing cases far more challenging than this one, he had been supremely confident that he had a winner in the woman who wasn't there. What had gone wrong?

It is not unusual for lawyers to question jurors, and vice versa, after the verdict has been announced, the jury dismissed, and the court adjourned. And so when this trial was over, the bewildered defense attorney waited outside the courthouse for the jurors to emerge. He confronted the first few he saw: How could you have found the man guilty when you weren't even sure his wife was dead? Hadn't everybody turned to look for her in the back of the courtroom?

"Yes," answered one of the jurors, "everybody except your client."

*　　*　　*

The theatrics and the surprise ending of this trial are not easily duplicated, but the final decision does serve to illustrate how unpredictable juries can be. No verdict is assured until it has been announced. In fact, in most trials there is much more uncertainty than in The Case of the Woman Who Wasn't There. The verdict, it is said, can go either way. For the jurors this means walking a path full of thorns and pitfalls as they struggle to reach a decision.

Jurors may deliberate for hours or for days or weeks, examining evidence, reviewing testimony, analyzing the judge's charge —discussing, arguing, negotiating. In a later chapter we will be considering in some detail what goes on behind the locked door of a jury room. Here the point we wish to make is that as long as there is doubt, there is drama. For the defendant, the lawyers, the judges, and the spectators, "waiting out the verdict" can turn into an agonizing experience. The longer the jury is out, the more unpredictable the verdict. And all the while the tension mounts. When it is finally released, in that climactic moment when the jury announces its decision, whatever that decision may be, it holds an element of surprise and shock. The ending of the story may not be satisfying to everyone, but it is powerful beyond any doubt.

*   *   *

But occasionally there is no real ending at all. In a criminal case a jury's verdict generally must be unanimous, and not every group of twelve very different people, confronted with contradictory testimony and conflicting claims, can reach the common agreement that a verdict must be. The jurors may at some point declare themselves hopelessly deadlocked. Perhaps the judge orders them to resume deliberations. They continue to argue for a while, only to find themselves no closer to a generally acceptable decision, until, finally, the judge reluctantly acknowledges their failure. They have become what is known as a hung jury —a jury unable to come to any agreement except to disagree. Even this, however, is an ending of sorts. It may indeed prove a true ending should the district attorney decide not to try the case a second time or should the judge decide to drop the charges, with either result allowing the defendant to go free. But if there is to be a second trial, both sides will have learned something from the first and the ending of one story becomes the beginning of another.

"DEMOCRACY'S WAY OF ADMINISTERING JUSTICE"

How the Jury System Began and What It Is Today

Fittingly enough, the roots of the jury system can be traced to ancient Greece, where the idea of democracy itself was born. Athenians, it has been said, were a nation of lawyers and a nation without lawyers. Rather than resolving their disagreements by dueling or fighting, they took them to the tribunals, their courts of justice, where they were required to act as their own attorneys.

It was up to the individual to set the judicial process in motion; the state could not take action itself. A case against a murderer, for example, had to be brought in by a kinsman of the person slain. But as early as the fourth century, B.C., cases in Athens were heard by jurors (called Areopagites), typical citizens, at

least thirty years old, whose duty it was to evaluate evidence and render a verdict.

The number of jurors for any one trial, all of whom were chosen by lot, may to us seem staggering—from 201 to 1,001, depending upon the nature of the case. The selection of the panel of jurors for each courthouse was made on the day of the trial and was ruled by five basic considerations: that each person in the pool of jurors should have an equal opportunity to serve; that in its composition every panel should be representative of the community, of the people in whose name it acted; that the identity of the jurors who were to hear a particular case should be unknown to anyone but themselves prior to the beginning of the actual trial; that no one should impersonate any juror selected; and that jurors who failed to appear in court should be denied their daily wages.

It is quite remarkable that the concerns of the Athenians are the very ones that govern the selection and supervision of juries today. Some 2,500 years ago measures were being taken to insure that juries were fairly chosen, that they spoke in and for the true voice of their community, that they were not subject to intimidation or bribery, and that they did their work efficiently and expeditiously. Later, we will look at the form in which these measures have survived in modern times. Now we merely note with admiration how aware the ancient Greeks were of the requirements of the democratic ideal and the weaknesses of men.

While the function of the Athenian jury and the precautions taken in its selection are familiar to us, many of the customs of the court of that age may seem strange indeed. Some of them reflect the values of the ancient Greek social order: slaves, for example, were permitted to testify only when under torture (otherwise, presumably, they would speak lies), and women and minors were permitted to testify only in murder cases. Other rules of trial procedure seem equally curious: the cross-examination of witnesses, which is so crucial in modern trials, was not allowed and thus statements in support of one side could not be challenged by the other; legal precedents—that is, decisions made in earlier similar disputes—were totally disregarded; and once the hearing was over, the jurors voted without deliberation or discussion on whether to acquit or condemn.

The last was no doubt unavoidable, given the number of jurors participating in any one trial. Certainly hundreds of voices would not make for orderly discourse. Nor could the jurors be expected to sound a unanimous vote. Decisions were by a simple majority in a secret ballot. (It is interesting to observe that prosecutors who failed to get at least one-fifth of the jurors' votes were compelled to pay a fine for having brought suit in the first place.) After a decision was reached, both parties to a suit, the loser as well as the winner, would suggest the penalty to be paid; and after listening to their respective arguments, the jurors would again vote, to decide whose recommendation was to be accepted.

The weaknesses of the Athenian jury system are almost self-evident, centering as they do on the large number of jurors participating in a trial. To imagine over 200 people hearing a case and making a judgment is to call to mind a scene more reminiscent of a carnival than a courtroom and a system of justice based more on the rule of the mob than the rule of law. Moreover, with the power of decision distributed among so many, the sense of responsibility of the individual juror (which, as we shall see, is crucial to the effectiveness of a jury today) had to be diluted and frail.

But the strengths of the system must also be acknowledged. Never before, and probably never again, was so large a proportion of common citizens to become familiar with and take part in legal practice. And, most important, the system was the essence of the democratic principle: large bodies of people, fairly chosen, taking collective action for the common good. Something *was* lost when the size of juries dwindled from 1,001 to 12.

Early European Jury Systems

With the collapse of the ancient Greek civilization, juries in the peculiar form known to the Athenians were lost forever. Nevertheless, the Athenians had established for all time the custom of using laymen, strangers to the law, to help decide matters of legal disagreement. In ancient Rome, where democracy eventually yielded to autocracy—the rule by dictatorship—the jury survived only as a select group of advisers to a magistrate. In this vague Roman form, embodied in a group of counselors or assistants to a figure of authority, the jury concept can later be found in northern, central and eastern Europe and in the Anglo-Saxon law of the Middle Ages.

But since, as the Greeks recognized, the jury system is both the symbol and the expression of democratic government, it was not until democracy took root in European soil that the jury as we know it began to emerge. After the Norman Conquest of England in 1066, Anglo-Saxon law was altered and enriched by the principles and practices of the French invaders, and slowly, over centuries, the jury was shaped into being. By the early thirteenth century in England a person accused of a serious crime was recognized to have the right to a jury trial, and by the middle of the eighteenth century, the institution was so deeply implanted that Sir William Blackstone, one of the greatest legal thinkers of all time, wrote of it in his *Commentaries,* "The liberties of England cannot but [continue] so long as this palladium remains sacred and inviolate."

From England the concept of the jury spread to Continental Europe. In 1748, in a book called *The Spirit of the Laws,* Montesquieu, whose thought and writings helped to spark the French Revolution, declared that the jury was "democracy's way of administering justice." One hundred years later, well after the French Revolution and following the political upheavals that swept Europe in the first half of the nineteenth century, the jury system had been established in France, Germany, Austria-Hungary, and other countries throughout the Continent—even, in 1864, in Czarist Russia.

But on the Continent, the jury system was modified in many important ways, all of which were intended to restrict the jurors' power. Clearly, many countries, then and now ruled by a more or less democratic form of government, were not content to let a group of laymen, totally unacquainted with the law, decide by themselves the issue of guilt and innocence when a person's fate and the safety of society were at stake. Knowledgeable professionals were considered essential in reaching a proper and just verdict. Thus, in the most extreme reaction to what is regarded as the great weakness of the jury system, Holland and Luxembourg eventually abandoned the system entirely, returning all powers of decision in a trial to the judge.

In most other European countries, over time, the role of the jury was substantially reduced while the role of the judge or, more likely, a panel of judges, was markedly enhanced. Judges were enabled to exert stronger influence on the jury's verdict by "instructing" the jurors to a much greater extent than the English system now allows. Judges were permitted to sit in on the jury's deliberations, and, most significantly of all, they were given the authority to set aside a jury's verdict if they thought it to be incorrect. Today, the mixed tribunal, a court in which power is shared between a larger number of jurors (but fewer than twelve) and a smaller number of judges, is the most prevalent type of trial arrangement throughout the European continent. In the Orient, outside of those countries that were once part of the British Empire, juries composed of laymen are virtually unknown. All trial power is vested in people of legal training and experience.

The Jury System in America

By far the most successful migration of the English model jury was across the Atlantic. While in New England the colonists of the seventeenth century generally did not feel bound by English common law—they had suffered too much from governmental tyranny for that—they did adopt the English concepts of property, liberty, and justice to the extent they considered them appropriate for a new life in a new land. The jury system was certainly one way for a people seeking freedom to curb the authority of the state. In the European countries, the jury system was grafted onto a tree of existing legal traditions. In some cases, as we have seen, the graft did not take at all, and the new limb eventually dropped off; in other cases, it shrank considerably in size. In the American colonies, however, the jury system was an integral part of the Tree of Liberty that was planted at the time of our nation's birth. As such, it has flourished here as it has nowhere else in the world.

*   *   *

Today at least 80 percent of all criminal jury trials worldwide take place in the United States. Not only is the system most deeply rooted here and most thoroughly accepted, but it also gives jurors more power—that is, more freedom of decision—than they are allowed in any other major nation. This power is simply the reverse side of the coin of responsibility, and in the United States the responsibility for achieving justice, like all other aspects of government, is derived from and rests with the people. The principle is so important to us that the right to trial by jury is preserved in our Constitution in both Article 3 and in the Sixth Amendment of the Bill of Rights, and it is guaranteed in every state constitution as well. Aside from voting in elections, where the impact of any one person's choice is weakened by the huge number of voters in the group, the jury system allows individuals more direct and effective expression of their will than any other institution we now have. Writing letters to congressmen, marching on the Pentagon, handing out leaflets on a street corner near the White House, and demonstrating in front of City Hall are all valid ways for us to make our views known and to influence the men and women we have elected to govern us. Such measures, however dramatic they may be, may or may not change anything. But the verdict of twelve people sitting in a small-town courthouse in Wyoming, having heard a case that is unpublicized and unknown outside of the community, may restore a man to his family or may take him from that family forever.

Why is the power, and the responsibility, of jurors greater in the United States than anywhere else? The jury system came to the United States with the first English colonists, but it responded to and was shaped by what is distinctly the American experience. From Westerns we all know about the "frontier justice" practiced by people living in settlements with only the beginnings of an organized legal system, or perhaps with none at all, who regularly "took the law into their own hands" and punished a presumed offender in whatever manner they saw fit. They couldn't wait for the judge who rode into town once every few months or so. Besides, they didn't necessarily trust that judge anyway.

There is in the American character a fundamental distrust or at least a suspicion of authority. Political leaders tend to be most revered after they have died or left office. And if in an increasingly complex society, ordinary people recognize that they must give to others ever greater control over their own daily lives, they are all the more apt to cherish and keep for themselves whatever power they legitimately can. One of the last strongholds of such power is in the jury box. There, average citizens, having no special qualifications of any kind, actively participate in the workings of one of the three chief branches of government, the judicial system. They can freely exercise their own judgment, and, to a truly extraordinary extent, they can still take the law into their own hands.

We have seen how in other countries trial power is divided between judges and jurors, with the former required to give strong direction to the deliberations of the latter. In United States criminal courts, there is not so much a sharing of power as a division of powers. The judge is supreme in determining how a trial is to proceed and what evidence will be permitted. The jury is supreme in determining the guilt or innocence of the accused. In this regard, the guidance jurors receive from a judge is minimal. While in most states a judge in his final charge to the jury is permitted to review and summarize the evidence that has been presented during the trial, in some states he may not even do that. In his charge, his authority is limited to instructing the jurors on the law in question and explaining the counts on which the defendant has been indicted. But the fact is that, in either case, after they have retired to the jury room to deliberate, the jurors may in effect choose to ignore—indeed, to defy—everything they have just been told.

To illustrate, let's imagine that in his charge a judge has gone into considerable detail in outlining a state law that prohibits most forms of gambling. While he has not discussed why the statute was passed, he has stressed that at this time and place it is beyond the jurors' function to question the wisdom of their state legislators in enacting such a law: It is "on the books" and therefore must be enforced. If the jury believes that the defendant has, as charged, broken this law by setting up and managing an illegal betting establishment, they must, the judge declares, find him guilty. Upon retiring to the jury room, the jurors begin their deliberations and all quickly agree that the defendant did in fact operate a betting parlor. He is then clearly guilty.

"But wait," says one juror. "Sure, this guy was running the bookie joint, but it was never absolutely proved that he owned it." When only two other jurors express doubt on this point, the first juror is forced to admit what really troubles him. "Okay," he says, "let's say he does own the place. So what? What real harm was the poor guy doing when he let those people place their lousy two buck bets?"

"Right!" says someone else, and in time all of the jurors conclude that the defendant was probably doing no great harm to anyone.

"Then why the hell convict him?" asks the first gadfly of a juror.

"Well, he did break the law," another juror remarks rather timidly.

"Sure," says the first juror, "but what about the guy who can take the day off to go to the track with two thousand bucks that his family really needs? He drops all of it by the last race and comes home without a dime. Does he get arrested? No, it's all perfectly legal."

Thus the jury has come upon an entirely new path, one that the judge certainly never intended these twelve people to follow —and, with some help from that vague doubt about the ownership of the betting parlor, the path leads almost inevitably to a verdict of not guilty.

Obviously, juries do not very often effectively repeal a law passed by a democratically elected legislature. But in what are sometimes called "political trials"—where the defendant's views on a controversial public issue assume an importance at least equal to the matter of his or her guilt—jury nullification of the law is not at all uncommon. During the Vietnam War, for example, men and women charged with destroying government property as part of their antiwar demonstrations were acquitted even though their burning of draft board records was beyond question. That jurors, in the face of decisive evidence to the contrary, should render not-guilty verdicts is a stunning commentary on the jury system. Whether that commentary is favorable or unfortunate is in itself a highly controversial issue among judges, attorneys, and students of the law, one that we will touch upon in a later chapter. For the moment, we must simply marvel at the power twelve ordinary people—strangers to one another and engaged in no conspiracy, not elected to any sort of office, and not educated in the ways of the law—can, under the right circumstances, command.

The Grand Jury

We have until now been describing the jury in criminal trials, the *petit jury,* and it is to this that the chapters that follow will be almost entirely devoted. However, in considering the development of the jury system in general, and its place in American justice in particular, we must mention an adaptation of the jury concept that originated in the United States and remains an almost exclusively American phenomenon. This adaptation is called the *grand jury.*

Like the petit jury, the grand jury is composed of laymen with no special legal background or training, people of all ages and from all walks of life. Also like the petit jury, the grand jury is empaneled to hear evidence and to make a judgment upon it. Members of both petit juries and grand juries are modestly paid for their services. But there the similarities between the two types of juries end.

A petit jury usually consists of twelve people but in recent years, more and more frequently, fewer.

A grand jury consists of at least six people but generally many more, up to a maximum of twenty-four.

A petit jury serves on one specific trial for as many consecutive days as it takes to hear all the evidence and reach a verdict. (Sometimes unavoidable circumstances cause the progress of a trial to be delayed for a day or more, but such interruptions are unforeseen, unusual, and highly irregular.)

A grand jury serves for an indefinite period that may extend for weeks, months, or even years, but it does not sit every day during that period and may be in session as infrequently as once a month; its work may relate to one case but more often relates to many cases.

A petit jury hears evidence and renders a verdict as to the guilt or innocence of a defendant.

A grand jury hears evidence and decides if the state—that is, the district attorney's office—has any grounds for believing that a person or persons might have committed a crime and thus should be brought to trial; its decision, if affirmative, is called an *indictment.*

A petit jury is involved in an *adversary proceeding*—that is, with defense and prosecution acting in opposition, each side trying to lead the jury to a conclusion that is exactly contrary to the other's.

A grand jury hears only the prosecution's side; the person who is the target of a grand jury inquiry may, under certain circumstances, testify at the hearing, but, depending upon state law, he either cannot be represented by an attorney at all or he can have an attorney present in the courtroom merely for the purpose of consultation.

As we shall see later, criticisms of the jury system persist, directed mainly at its very foundation: the practice of giving laymen who know little or nothing about the law the power of legal decision. Such criticisms apply more or less equally to both the petit and the grand jury. But in addition, and increasingly in recent years, the grand jury alone has been subject to certain stinging attacks on its methods and objectives.

Historically, the grand jury was created to act as a bulwark between the state and the potential defendant—to insure that a hapless individual would not be prosecuted without probable cause. In effect, the grand jury was meant to introduce an element of democratic action into a legal proceeding at the earliest possible moment—either when a crime is merely suspected, or immediately after a person has been arrested and before he has been formally charged with any wrongdoing. Members of a grand jury are thus investigators of a sort, empowered to determine, first, whether it appears that a crime has been committed and, second, whether it is likely that a particular person (or persons) committed it. Having ordinary representatives of the community, speaking for the community, make such judgments would appear to be a commendable expression of the democratic principle. However, in actual fact, critics charge, the methods followed at most grand jury hearings are a violation of democratic practices: since only one side, the prosecution, presents any evidence, the scope of the jurors' investigation is severely limited, with the result, experience has shown, that rarely do the jurors deny to a district attorney the indictment he seeks. The grand jury system thus has been characterized as a rubber stamp for the state, a tool the district attorney uses to put the community's apparent seal of approval on an action that, in truth, has not been fairly weighed or tested by anyone outside of his office.

It can, of course, be argued that if a grand jury is mistaken in handing up an indictment, its error will be rectified when the accused person goes to trial. True enough, but unfortunately in most communities today there is such a backlog of cases awaiting court action that the time between a defendant's indictment and trial is almost certain to stretch for months and may indeed extend over more than a year. During that period if a defendant has been released without bail or has succeeded in raising the bail the court has set, he is, for all intents and purposes, free although under indictment. But if a defendant is unable to raise bail, he spends the time between indictment and trial behind bars, in effect serving an indeterminate sentence before he has been convicted of any crime. Should the defendant eventually be tried, found guilty, and sentenced, the time he has already served is usually subtracted from his prison term. Should he be tried and found not guilty, the time he has served remains a debt owed to him by society that can never be repaid. Thus, there is no denying that the consequences of a grand jury error may not only be serious but irreversible—that is, to some extent, beyond remedy.

Suppose grand juries did not exist. A district attorney's office could indict people on its own without any kind of approval from the community, symbolic or otherwise. No doubt more indictments would be handed up, although probably not very many more; certainly the substantial costs of grand jury proceedings would be saved; but, most important, an element of pretense in our judicial system would be eliminated. The very idea of democracy is cheapened when a custom claimed to be democratic, and which seems on the surface to be democratic, is proved to be essentially arbitrary and one-sided.

Civil Trials

So speak the critics of the grand jury system. They are no more vehement than those who attack the use of petit juries for a category of trials that we have not so far touched upon. This book is for the most part concerned with criminal trials, but many petit juries serve on trials where the commission of a crime is not at all at issue. What is at issue is the charge by one party, called the *plaintiff,* that he has been physically injured or that his property has been damaged or that he has been wronged in some other way by a second party, the *defendant,* who is now being sued for damages. Lawsuits such as this are, more often than not, settled out of court by negotiations between attorneys representing the two sides. If the disputes make it to court, agreement may be reached there with judicial aid and encouragement, or, as a last resort, they may become the bases for what are known as *civil,* as opposed to criminal, trials.

In a civil trial, the plaintiff's lawyer plays much the same role as the prosecutor does in a criminal trial. He is out to prove to the jury that the defendant committed an offense against his client. (In criminal trials, offenses may or may not be against individuals. They may be against the state, as in cases of tax fraud.) The defendant's lawyer, of course, tries to prove just the opposite. And the jury must decide not only which side is right, but also, if it finds in favor of the plaintiff, the amount of money the defendant must pay for having committed the offense.

Money. Practically speaking, that spells the basic difference between criminal trials and civil trials.

What is at stake in a criminal jury trial? In 1970, in a highly controversial decision, the Supreme Court ruled that the right to a jury trial may be reserved for crimes that carry a sentence of more than six months in prison. Whatever one may think of this ruling—and criticism of it is deep and widespread—it means that for the defendant in a criminal jury trial, conviction holds the threat, at the very least, of taking a small portion of his life and, at the very most, all of it. For the community, the outcome of a trial may provide a measure of protection against possible future crimes and satisfaction of the inescapable need to exact punishment for wrongdoing.

What is at stake in a civil jury trial? To a very limited extent, elements of all the above. Certainly a defendant in a civil trial may risk damage to his reputation or to his means of livelihood, and the community stands to gain from learning about such things as the negligence of a physician or the tainted food served by a restaurant owner. But what is mainly at stake in almost all civil trials is money: will the defendant, or, quite often, his insurance company, have to pay, and how much?

This is not meant to suggest that civil trials are unimportant or even undramatic. Some fairly recent civil trials that warranted mention in the press include:

A man in California, who was paralyzed from the waist down when his car turned over, sued Volkswagen of America, Inc., for $500,000, only to have the jury decide—after a twenty-day trial —that the United States distributor was not responsible for the injury. Presumably the jury accepted the auto manufacturer's contention that its car was as safe as any other model sports car of that year.

A woman in Michigan lost a $1-million damage suit against a hospital that she claimed had given her the wrong baby after her delivery eight years earlier. The six-member jury deliberated for almost seven hours before deciding that, on the basis of the evidence, she had gotten the right baby after all.

A man in Minnesota was awarded $5,040 because city officials did not wait long enough to kill his cat. The cat had run away from home, was captured by the police after it frightened a rabbit to death, and was slain by a shotgun blast three hours later at the police station, which had no facilities for keeping cats. The four men and two women on the jury made the award to the plaintiff after deciding that the police had violated a city ordinance requiring that pets be held for five days before being killed.

A professor in New York was awarded more than half a million dollars when a jury decided that college officials had violated his right to free speech and association. He contended, and the jury agreed, that he had been denied promotion and tenure only because he had once given information to the Central Intelligence Agency.

These cases, chosen at random but to illustrate a point, offer some indication of how varied are the nature of civil lawsuits and, consequently, how varied are the judgments juries in such lawsuits are expected to make. By far the greatest number of civil cases stem from charges of negligence—on the part of automobile drivers, landlords, physicians, repairmen, and just about everyone else. Like the Volkswagen distributor, the hospital, and the city and college officials in the cases cited above, all these defendants are being sued for damages, and, taken together, their cases demand of juries a breadth of knowledge, an attention to detail, and a sense of fairness that few if any of us would ever pretend to.

Much of the criticism that has been leveled against the jury system—charges of bias, ignorance, inattention, and the like that we will consider at length in our final chapter—applies with particular force to juries in civil trials. Attacks have come not only from plaintiffs and defendants, but also from lawyers and judges up to and including the Chief Justice of the United States, Warren E. Burger.

It is said that in criminal trials, most jurors bring to their jobs a deep sense of personal responsibility, a recognition of the seriousness of the occasion, a determination to act wisely because so much is at stake. But, critics hold, civil trial jurors tend to minimize their own shortcomings, to indulge their own prejudices, and to play with the facts of a case in a game called "Money." Neither the attitude expressed by "Let the insurance company pay through the nose; they can afford it," nor the reverse, "People are always trying to collect for every little fracture," is conducive to the just and honorable resolution of civil suits.

Recognizing this, attorneys in civil suits often play a game of their own. They announce, usually many years after the incident in question occurred, that they are ready to argue their case before a jury. In time, a jury is empaneled—but it never gets to deliberate. Sometimes before the jurors have even taken an oath, sometimes after they have been sworn in, sometimes before they have heard any witnesses, sometimes during or just after the presentation of evidence, they are abruptly sent back to the jury room and later recalled to the courtroom only to be thanked for their services and dismissed. What has happened? The case has been settled out of court.

In effect, each side in the dispute has dared the other to allow those six or eight or twelve strangers to resolve the disagreement, and one side or the other, or perhaps both, has decided that it had better not take such a chance.

For jurors who have been used in this way, the experience is indelible and exasperating. And thus, the loudest cries against the use of juries in civil cases probably come from the jurors themselves. No one likes to serve as a pawn in other people's games.

WHO'S ON TRIAL HERE?

How a Jury Is Chosen

If you are of voting age and have voted, paid taxes, and managed to stay out of serious trouble with the law, the chances are good that someday you will be called for jury duty. Federal and state laws on juror qualifications differ considerably, as do the practices of the various courts that actually summon citizens to serve. Obviously, with enormous differences among localities in population and crime rate come equally great differences in their need for jurors. A longtime resident of an urban center is more likely to be called than a recently arrived resident of a suburb; and during their lifetimes both will probably serve more often than someone who lives in a rural area. And just as the rules of eligibility and the extent of need vary from place to place, they also, and very decidedly, change with the times—that is, with the gradual but continuous evolution of social values.

Thus, years ago in many states women were never "drafted" for jury duty; if they wished to become jurors they could volunteer, but they were under no legal obligation to serve. That is no longer the case. Laws permitting the automatic exemption of women were declared unconstitutional by the United States Supreme Court in 1975, in a ruling that emphasized the defendant's right to an impartial jury selected from a true cross section of his community. In theory, this ruling spelled the end of the underrepresentation not only of women (whose membership in the pool of qualified jurors in New York City, for example, between 1975 and 1978 jumped from 18 percent to 45 percent) but of all minority groups that had been *systematically* excluded from jury service. The Supreme Court decision was a giant step toward the ancient Athenian objective of a jury panel genuinely representative of the people in whose name it acted.

In pursuit of the same ideal, recent years have seen the end of automatic jury exemption for certain occupations and types of employment. In some states, schoolteachers, for example, were never called, and in many places the self-employed were excused simply because they were self-employed. No more. Perhaps the only generally exempt professions left are medicine and, needless to say, law.

But if the ranks of the eligible have now been expanded to include almost everyone, what mechanism is used to determine exactly who will be asked to serve? It should come as no surprise that in most states today modern technology's great gift to us all, the computer, does the job. First it searches through the names of all the persons in the community who are qualified, names taken chiefly from voter registration lists and tax rolls, choosing those who have never before been summoned for jury duty. It is further programmed to scan the lists of people who have already served and to give preference in selection to those whose service was longest ago. In other words, the more recently you have served, the less likely it is that you will be called again.

Of course, mistakes are made, but they can usually be corrected without too much difficulty. A notice of jury service indicates a date, hour, and place for you to appear. At that time, or even before, you are given an opportunity to explain why you cannot or should not be asked to serve. If just a few months earlier you were on jury duty for at least the customary two-week period, you are not apt to have any trouble convincing a court officer that it's unfair for you to be called so soon again. The chances are, however, that if you wish to be excused it will be for a reason other than that, and, generally speaking, you will find the court understanding. Don't expect to be excused from jury duty *forever,* but do expect to have your service postponed, perhaps even to a time that you specify as being more convenient for you.

Postponements will be granted for all sorts of clearly legitimate reasons: a field has to get plowed, an exam has to be taken, a baby has to get born, a meeting has to be attended, a sick child

CALDWELL

has to be cared for, a movie has to be made. Courts are aware that many obligations cannot be broken without causing serious loss of income or other hardship. But, occasionally, people try to get out of jury duty by offering reasons of another sort altogether. For example:

"I'm against capital punishment."

"I think all the cops in this town are corrupt."

"I know from experience that all lawyers are crooks."

Regardless of whether such opinions are sincerely held or temporarily adopted, don't bother to express them in order to get excused from jury service. At best any one of them may keep you off the jury in a particular trial. But even if they are profoundly heartfelt, they are irrelevant to your suitability for the jury *pool.* However peculiar your views and prejudices may be, the court, at least in theory, can find a place for you in a jury box where they will do no harm.

In the Waiting Room

Having taken a seat in the waiting room, you find yourself surrounded by hundreds of other prospective jurors, and you quickly come to the conclusion that in two weeks, the usual "tour of duty" in most courts, there could not possibly be a sufficient number of trials to require the services of everyone in the group. No doubt you will be proved right. Although needs vary sharply from court to court, it is not uncommon for a person to complete jury duty without ever having heard a case. It *is* rare for a person not even to be summoned to a courtroom during a two-week stint. But as we shall see, particularly in a criminal court, there is a vast difference between being questioned for a jury and being chosen for one. Your jury duty experience may well turn into a series of rejection notices, so that when it is over you will have decided nothing more crucial than where to have lunch each day or whether to read a book or solve crossword puzzles. And to make matters worse, it is not *impossible* that you will never leave the waiting room.

The reasons for the apparently excessive number of prospective jurors are at least threefold.

First, when a court sends out its commands to report for jury duty, it cannot predict exactly (although experience allows it to estimate) how many of the people receiving them will be able to serve. It must allow for a certain number of "no-shows" and legitimate exemptions and, therefore, will summon many more people than it needs.

Second, a court's need for jurors during any one period will change according to disruptions in its calendar—the schedule of cases to be heard and tried—and this, too, is somewhat unpredictable. A trial may be set for a certain date only to be postponed because a crucial witness has disappeared or an attorney has fallen ill. A trial that was expected to be completed in five days may drag on for three weeks. A scheduled civil case may suddenly be settled out of court. Jurors are called on the basis of *anticipated* court needs—for a heavy calendar more will be summoned than for a light calendar—but, as we all know, the anticipated does not always happen.

Finally, there is one place where what appears to be an excessive number of jurors eventually proves to be an illusion—in the courtroom. There, inevitably, many prospective jurors will be challenged—that is, rejected from service—in the process of empaneling a jury for a particular trial. The specific reasons for challenge are many and various, as we shall see, but more often than not a prospective juror is excused because the defense, the prosecution, or the judge—or any combination of the three—believes the person could not maintain the necessary objectivity and fairness in considering the case at hand.

Nowadays, if only because of soaring crime rates, most crimes are *not* highly publicized—indeed, most receive no newspaper, radio, or television mention at all. But when a case does explode on the front pages and the nightly news shows, either locally or nationally (two recent examples of the latter are the Patty Hearst case in San Francisco and the "Son of Sam" case in New York), empaneling a jury becomes a court's nightmare. It seems that everyone has read or heard about such cases, and almost everyone has formed an opinion about the guilt or innocence of the accused. Finding jurors who will even claim to be open-minded and who will then appear to verify this under questioning becomes a Herculean task. (If a case has generated considerable press and television coverage in a particular locality, the defense attorney may petition the court for a *change of venue*—that is, the moving of the trial to another place in the state. There it should be easier to find twelve people who, knowing little or nothing about the crime, are more apt to show impartiality.) It is, of course, the hugely publicized cases that may go through literally hundreds or even thousands of prospects before twelve jurors and a few alternates are at last selected. The size of the jury pool must take this into account since it would be unthinkable for a trial to be delayed while more prospective jurors were summoned from home and from work.

A Courtroom at Last

So there you are, waiting. It is your third or fourth day. You have yet to be called for a trial. Other people have been going off to courtrooms in large groups, but the vast majority of them have soon straggled back, most of them disappointed, all of them rejected.

Now a telephone rings on a desk at the front of the room. The sound shatters the lethargy that has settled over everyone. People look up expectantly. A court officer answers, listens, puts down the receiver, and walks over to the "drum," a large, rotating metal container that holds the names of all the prospective jurors. He twirls the drum, reaches inside for a fat handful of cards, and begins to read off names. Fortune has finally smiled on you: yours is among them.

The number of winners in this lottery is determined by the kind of trial for which a jury is to be chosen. If the defendant is charged with a misdemeanor—that is, with a less serious crime such as simple assault or petty larceny—perhaps fifteen to twenty names will be called. If the trial is for a felony—that is, a more serious crime such as aggravated assault, grand larceny, or murder—as many as fifty people may be asked to step forward. After all of you have assembled at the front of the room, you may be told the name of the judge to whose courtroom you are about

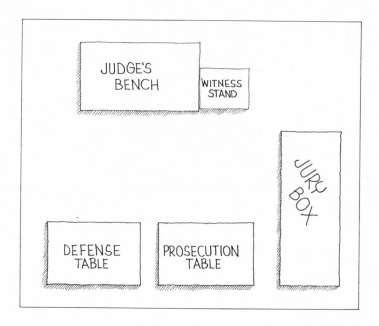

to be escorted and the crime of which the person on trial has been accused. If you do not know these things as a guard leads you down the halls, you will find them out soon enough.

In the courtroom you are seated at the rear, in the spectators section, directly facing the judge's bench. The jury box, now empty, is at one side down in front. At a right angle to it is the defense table, at which sit the defendant and counsel; next to them is the prosecutor's desk.

The judge introduces himself to the prospective jurors, identifies the attorneys and the defendant, and describes, in a general rather than a detailed way, the offense of which the defendant is accused, stating the time and place the crime occurred and the name of the victim if there was one. He estimates how long the trial is likely to last. Then he asks if anyone in your group is related to or knows personally any of the principals in the case, lives in the immediate vicinity of the crime, or is aware of other reasons he or she should not even be considered for the jury. He may even ask if anybody feels incapable of resisting group pressure, of holding fast to an opinion in defiance of all those around you.

If the judge has predicted that the trial will take three weeks and it would be a severe hardship for you to serve that long, if the assistant district attorney is your sister-in-law, if the trial is for murder and the victim was your gardener, if you can't tolerate conflict and always give in to others, now is your chance to speak up and probably be excused. Back to the jurors waiting room you will go, but that is the proper place for you if, at this early point, you suspect that you cannot be the reasonably impartial, attentive, cooperative, and responsible juror that the law demands.

Perhaps then your ranks have been thinned a bit as now a court officer, upon instructions from the judge, draws names from another drum, which contains cards for everyone remaining in your group. In one common procedure (though it has many variations), the names of four or five are called and these people are asked to take the first seats in the jury box. The jury selection process has begun. What follows is the examination, the questioning, of the potential jurors.

Surviving the Voir Dire

It is called the *voir dire,* derived from old French and literally meaning "to speak truly." Out of this procedure eventually emerge the twelve jurors required in most criminal cases (today civil cases often use smaller juries though never of fewer than six) and one to four alternates. (These alternates, during the course of the trial, may become regular jurors if any of the latter, for whatever reason, cannot continue to serve.) Those who are chosen are the "survivors," people who have managed to answer a barrage of questions without gravely displeasing the judge, the defense attorney, or the prosecutor—a task not easily performed.

What are these three looking for in a juror? Unfortunately for the person who is eager to serve, they are all not seeking the same qualities. The judge wants someone who is relatively unbiased, who will weigh the evidence carefully and intelligently, and who is capable of understanding certain basic principles of law and justice. He is particularly concerned about one principle, a mighty foundation of our legal system that should be known to all of us even before we enter the courthouse: *In the United States a person accused of a crime is presumed innocent until proved guilty.*

In a recent survey of the public's familiarity with and attitudes toward the courts, an astonishing 37 percent of the participants thought exactly the opposite—that the defendant was responsible for *proving his innocence.* Judges, aware that this misconception exists, will almost always explain to prospective jurors when they arrive in the courtroom—that is, before the *voir dire* even begins —that *the burden of proof rests on the prosecution.* If a jury is to return a verdict of guilty, the district attorney must *prove* the defendant's guilt beyond a reasonable doubt. Not beyond *all* doubt, but beyond a reasonable doubt—there is a significant distinction. If the district attorney fails to accomplish this, the jury must find the defendant innocent.

This principle has not been adopted throughout the world, but it applies in every legal jurisdiction, large and small, in the United States. While it is of course explained at all criminal trials —usually a multitude of times—hearing it, lawyers have found, is not always believing it.

In any courtroom in this country during a *voir dire* you will hear people say things like:

"I kind of figure that the defendant wouldn't be here in the first place if there wasn't a pretty good case against him."

"Well, yes, I would be bothered if you [the defense lawyer] didn't *prove* that your client was innocent."

"I don't see why the D.A. has to demonstrate guilt and you [the defense lawyer] can get away with just tearing his case to pieces."

"Sure, I'd be influenced if the defendant didn't take the stand. He has to convince me that he didn't do it."

Statements like these betray a deep-seated, perhaps unshakeable, though unconscious, belief in the presumption of guilt. To hold to such a belief after one has been instructed to the contrary is evidence of a stubborn prejudgment, an opinion formed before hearing all the facts—in a word, a prejudice.

Judge, defense attorney, and prosecutor alike are seeking out the prejudices of the prospective jurors, this particular prejudice and others as well; but only the judge is in pursuit of the ideal —an absence of all prejudices, complete impartiality. It is doubtful that he ever finds it, and as long as human beings report for jury duty, it is doubtful that he ever will. But it is on the judge that the system must rely to uncover the most potentially dangerous prejudices and to see that those infected with them do not become jurors.

In *their* search for prejudices, the defense and prosecution are less concerned with impartiality. Recognizing as they do that any one of us is a tangled mass of irrationality—of likes and dislikes, of attractions and suspicions, of trusts and distrusts—they set out to find in each prospective juror those prejudices that are likely to be harmful or helpful to their respective positions. The defense attorney insists, above all, that any juror selected have a genuine belief in the presumption of innocence. For him this is essential, not simply because the principle is a pillar of American law, but, far more practically, because holding to the principle is of invaluable benefit to his client. Finding twelve or more people who he believes will look favorably upon the defendant, who will judge his client sympathetically, is the defense attorney's overriding objective. The reverse of this coin is, of course, that he is intent on exposing and rooting out prospective jurors who might be hostile to the defendant.

Turn all that around and you have the goal of the prosecuting attorney: to place on the jury people he feels will look with disfavor on the defendant, and to keep off those who he suspects will show excessive tolerance.

If the objectives of the attorneys seem elementary and unsurprising, they are. What may be shocking, however, especially to someone who has never observed a *voir dire,* are the methods lawyers sometimes use to attain their ends.

Prospective jurors are after all ordinary citizens, generally law-abiding, who have, probably reluctantly, responded to a summons to participate in an activity that they know little about and for wages they no doubt regard as beneath contempt. Many of them would say they have better things to do than carry out this rather irksome responsibility the state has forced upon them. If they are not going to be showered with praise and gratitude merely for showing up at the courthouse, if, indeed, they are mostly to be left to languish, ignored and seemingly forgotten in a barren basement room, the very least prospective jurors should be able to expect when they *are* noticed is to be treated with courtesy, respect, and deference. In fact, once they step into the jury box to be interrogated, they may find themselves objects of suspicion and attack.

Lawyers will often say that a case can be won or lost when a jury is chosen, that the kinds of people the jurors are—their views and their values, their personalities and their temperaments—play a more influential role in determining the final verdict than does any of the evidence presented. For each side, then, selecting a "good" jury—that is, a jury that is thought to tilt, however slightly, in the direction the lawyer would like it to go —becomes a matter of enormous significance. In a recent, highly publicized trial the defense spent many thousands of dollars on a computer analysis of the objective facts about the prospective jurors—name, address, occupation, etc.—that had been furnished by the court. The defense attorney was then guided in his selection of jurors by the conclusions suggested by the computer report. He won the case.

What gives a lawyer the right to be so discriminating in choosing a jury? Aware that people are inclined to make prejudgments in all aspects of life, the framers of our legal system decreed that not only the judge, but the opposing lawyers as well, be allowed to try to uncover the prejudices of prospective jurors—thus, the *voir dire*—and, if they succeed, to try to prevent those people from sitting on the jury. For the latter purpose two weapons exist, the *challenge for cause* and the *peremptory challenge.*

The challenge for cause belongs exclusively to the judge. Since he is assumed to be neutral in the trial, as well as wise in all things, he can exercise challenges without restraint, excusing prospective jurors by the dozens, by the scores, by the hundreds, as he sees fit.

The peremptory challenge is the lawyer's alone. It confers on defense and prosecution the right to reject a prospective juror for any reason or for no apparent reason at all. The district attorney does not like redheads—he can keep them off the jury. The defense attorney distrusts Italians—he can send them all back to the waiting room. Actually, in exercising peremptory challenges a lawyer is not likely to be guided by whim, as these two examples suggest. But he may certainly act on intuition or, let's say, a gut feeling that a particular prospective juror would be unsympathetic to his case.

A peremptory challenge is a discharge without *stated* cause; it requires neither explanation or justification *of any kind.* And it is potentially so powerful a weapon that the legal system has placed restrictions on its use. In any trial, defense and prosecution are permitted a set and usually equal number of peremptory challenges. In misdemeanor cases there may be as few as three, while in felony cases the number generally falls between ten and twenty-five; it varies significantly with the nature of the felony charged—in a murder trial more peremptory challenges are permitted than in a burglary trial—and with the court and the state in which the trial takes place.

Because of these limits, it is decidedly to a lawyer's advantage to have his weeding-out work done for him by the judge. Remember that the latter has at his disposal an infinite number of challenges for cause. So it becomes the lawyer's mission to demonstrate to the judge that a particular prospective juror is not fit to serve on the jury. Each time he succeeds in this and persuades the judge to discharge the "suspect," he has saved a precious peremptory challenge—one that he can later use to get rid of a saint if he so chooses.

In exercising their power over jury selection, attorneys must proceed cautiously but penetratingly. While the *voir dire* may turn into something quite different, it usually starts as a dignified and friendly affair. After the judge has made his statement and asked his questions, the lawyers take over, beginning their interrogations with a smile and polite pleasantries like, "Hi, there! How are you today?"—greetings that are, if nothing else, designed to put the prospective juror at ease. But as you reply, the attorney is already taking your measure. From the card that was drawn from the drum he has learned certain basic information about you—your name, residence, occupation, at least—and

from your appearance and manner he learns a good deal more. Indeed, he may know all he needs to know.

No doubt it will seem to you shockingly unjust that in this place of justice you may be condemned to peremptory challenge before you have spoken a single word. But lawyers have very little time to question each prospective juror. The judge will not allow them to dawdle. They are therefore prone to come to instant conclusions about the strangers they confront, conclusions based on their own "experience," which may well be a string of prejudices in a professional disguise. To illustrate:

For a defense attorney—if you are elderly and live in a crime-ridden neighborhood, you are not wanted on a jury that will be hearing the case of an eighteen-year-old accused of mugging a sixty-five-year-old nurse; if you are a white storekeeper you are not wanted for the trial of a black woman charged with shoplifting.

For the prosecutor—if you are male and young and black, you are not wanted to determine the guilt of a defendant who is also male and young and black, whatever the crime for which he has been indicted; and if you are middle-aged, look Irish, and have an Irish-sounding name, you are not wanted to sit in judgment of Pat O'Rourke, forty-five, arrested for assault in a barroom brawl.

These examples, of course, are shamelessly vulnerable to the charge of stereotyped thinking, but the snap judgments lawyers make about prospective jurors reek of stereotyped thinking. There are no statistics proving that a white storekeeper could not fairly and impartially weigh the evidence against a black defendant and come to a valid conclusion about her innocence of guilt. Nevertheless, lawyers believe it imperative that they think in this short-circuit way. It's a form of playing the law of averages, a reliance on the odds of human nature. And it is hard to imagine that anyone in the same position would think and act more democratically or more scientifically.

Nor does short-circuit thinking end when the actual questions begin. The replies lawyers receive trigger in them certain set responses, warnings that the person would not be sympathetic or, less often, indications that he or she would be. For example, let's consider five popular *voir dire* questions and show in a chart how both defense and prosecution would react to five possible answers.

The questions are:
1. Did you have any education beyond high school?
2. How old are your children?
3. Have you recently been, or are you close to anyone who has recently been, the victim of a crime?
4. What newspaper do you read?
5. Do you believe that policemen are capable of dishonesty and could lie under oath?

Answer	Defense Reaction	Prosecution Reaction
1. Graduated from college	+	−
2. Has a child of eighteen	+	−
3. Aunt was mugged a year ago	−	+
4. Reads a newspaper that has a generally liberal editorial slant	+	−
5. Police have been known to be corrupt and to lie	+	−

While no one of the above answers would necessarily prove fatal to a person's chances of serving on a jury, taken together, in most cases involving criminal violence, they would set off an alarm in the mind of the prosecution. Of course, the facts of a particular trial do govern the thinking of *both* lawyers.

Let us assume that a twenty-year-old male, brought up in poverty, is on trial for attempted robbery and that the five answers were given by a woman approaching middle age. In the legal profession, conventional wisdom has it that:

1. College graduates tend to be more sympathetic to defendants, and women especially are more likely to be compassionate if an accused male has had a "hard life." (Interestingly enough, there is disagreement among lawyers as to whether women are as compassionate toward female defendants.)

2. Having a child of approximately the same age as the defendant may cause the juror to identify the two in her own mind.

3. Having been more or less directly victimized by a crime makes for a much "tougher" juror.

4. Reading a liberal newspaper suggests a more liberal thinker, a definite plus for the defense in most criminal trials.

5. Finally, and most important, if the police are going to be key witnesses for the prosecution—as they so often are in criminal cases—a tendency to see them as anything but true-blue, upright, and thoroughly honest could be highly dangerous for the district attorney.

Thus, although our prospective juror, at least on the basis of these answers, would be acceptable to the defense attorney—and even he would be concerned about that mugged aunt—the prosecutor would almost certainly use one of his peremptory challenges to be rid of her. No one could argue that he has gotten to know the woman well, but who would doubt that he has learned enough for him to be wary of her?

So far the questioning has been matter-of-fact, courteous, inoffensive. Now let us imagine a gradual intensifying of the dialogue. The defendant in the trial is still the twenty-year-old male accused of attempted robbery, the prospective juror is still the woman approaching middle age. The questioner is the prosecutor, who has already decided this probable "bleeding heart" should not sit on the jury but who senses that she could be "persuaded" to force the judge to the same conclusion.

Prosecutor: You say that police may lie. Has any policeman ever lied to you that you know of?

Prospective Juror: No.

Prosecutor: Then why do you say that?

Prospective Juror: Because I've read in the newspapers of many cases where policemen tell half-truths or embroider the truth to make themselves look good.

Prosecutor: Have you read anything at all about this case in the press, or seen anything on television?

Prospective Juror: No.

Prosecutor: You heard from the judge that the defendant was stopped by the police and arrested a few blocks from the scene of the crime.

Prospective Juror: Yes.

Prosecutor: If a police officer testifies that he saw the defendant running from the scene of the crime, then saw him fling something into the bushes, and that "something" later turned out to be a gun, would you believe the officer who said this?

Prospective Juror: I'm not sure.

Prosecutor (his voice rising slightly): You're not sure?

Prospective Juror: No, I'm not sure.

Prosecutor: Why aren't you sure? Because you've read in the papers that police sometimes lie?

Prospective Juror: Not only that. I know it's the police's job to solve crimes and to do this they sometimes jump to conclusions that aren't so.

Prosecutor: For example?

Prospective Juror: Well, after the policeman found the gun in the bushes he may have just *thought* he saw the defendant throw it there because that would solve his case.

Prosecutor: You're suggesting that he didn't really see the defendant throw the gun in the bushes?

Prospective Juror: Yes, I am, or maybe the defendant threw something else.

Prosecutor: Something else. So now you're a detective! What might this "something else" be?

Prospective Juror: Oh, I don't know. Maybe an empty bottle.

Prosecutor: An empty bottle! Are you suggesting that a policeman couldn't tell the difference between a gun and an empty bottle?

Prospective Juror: Maybe he didn't see the boy throw anything but made that up after the gun was found.

Prosecutor: So you are saying that he *could* be lying?

Prospective Juror: I've said that from the beginning.

Prosecutor: So you have. Is there anything that would convince you the policeman wasn't lying?

Prospective Juror: If someone else saw him throw the gun—but not another policeman.

Prosecutor: Not another policeman. Why not another policeman?

Prospective Juror: Because he would also have a reason for lying.

Prosecutor (furiously): Do you really think that the policemen of this city go around lying and arresting innocent people because they want to solve crimes?

Prospective Juror: I believe some of them do, yes.

Prosecutor: Is there anything at all that could convince you the defendant threw the gun?

Prospective Juror: Well, I guess if his fingerprints were found on it. . . .

Prosecutor: When he was arrested he was wearing gloves.

Prospective Juror: Oh. Well, if the gun was registered in his name. . . .

Prosecutor: Registered in his name? Are you serious? Do you think people commit robberies with registered guns?

Prospective Juror: I don't know that much about it.

Prosecutor: You certainly don't.

Prospective Juror: If it could be proved that he bought the gun.

Prosecutor: And anything less than that would leave you thinking the policeman was lying.

Prospective Juror: Could be lying.

Prosecutor: What do you mean by that?

Prospective Juror: I'd have doubts as to whether he saw the boy throw the gun or not.

Prosecutor: What kind of doubts?

Prospective Juror: Oh, I don't know . . . doubts.

Prosecutor: You know from what the judge has told you that in order to convict the defendant you must find him guilty beyond a reasonable doubt?

Prospective Juror: Yes.

Prosecutor: Would you say that the sworn testimony of a police officer who has been on the force for fifteen years, has been decorated for heroism several times, and has never had a black mark against him could—all by itself—leave you with a reasonable doubt as to its accuracy?

Prospective Juror (after a long pause): I'm not sure.

Prosecutor: What does that mean—"I'm not sure"?

Prospective Juror: Well, when you start asking me about kinds of doubt, *degrees* of doubt. . . .

Prosecutor: Madam, believe me, I'm not asking you these questions just to stump you. Our job is not simply to solve crimes but to keep criminals off the streets, to protect people like you. And if you can't answer a simple question—

Prospective Juror: It's not a simple question.

Prosecutor: Then let me ask you this. Could this fine officer—and don't forget he has an impeccable record—could his testimony leave you with *greater* than a reasonable doubt?

Prospective Juror: Probably not.

Prosecutor: With *less* than a reasonable doubt?

Prospective Juror: I'm not sure.

Prosecutor (shouting): Again "I'm not sure"!

Prospective Juror: Well, of course, I haven't heard the testimony, but I guess I wouldn't want to have any doubt at all.

Prosecutor (softly): No doubt at all. I see. (Turning to the judge) Your honor, I move that the court challenge this woman for cause.

The judge so rules. The prosecutor has saved a peremptory challenge. The woman leaves the jury box shaken but with her integrity intact.

This sample of the type of interrogation a prospective juror may well experience demonstrates several pertinent points about how juries are selected.

First of all, it shows that dangers may lie beneath the surface of an apparently harmless opinion. When our embattled prospective juror expresses some doubt about police veracity, she is revealing a *kind* of prejudgment though a rather indefinite one. She is merely saying that the officer *could possibly* lie, not that he *would certainly* lie (which would of course prompt an immediate challenge by the judge). But—and this is the second point to note—once the prosecutor uncovers this prejudgment, he probes it and enlarges it, like a dentist exploring a cavity, until it is made to appear as a spot of decay in the woman's thinking.

Next, we should observe that to accomplish this the prosecutor uses increasingly aggressive tactics—expressing almost horrified disbelief at her answers (either genuine or pretended—the effect is the same), mocking the prospective juror, belittling her, lecturing her, always pressing her. The woman, who has been called to perform a public service and is eager to do so, is treated like an opponent. Indeed, to the prosecutor she *is* an opponent, and, in a sense, he is out to destroy her. He succeeds completely in that he both keeps her off the jury and avoids wasting a challenge on her. He has the judge finish her off instead.

When, finally badgered and battered, the woman admits that

she wants no doubt at all, she has been forced into a confession that is fatal. The law has decreed that in order to convict, the state must offer proof beyond a reasonable doubt, nothing more than that. This is the established rule and people who refuse to accept the rules must be barred from playing the game.

Others must be barred also—those who seem too slow-witted to be expected to understand all the evidence, those who have physical problems that might prevent them from sitting comfortably for hours, those who have defects of hearing or sight. You would think that such people would acknowledge their frailties before they were questioned and thereby save the court precious time. But some of us refuse to see ourselves as we really are and many of us are enraptured with the idea of serving on a jury. Keeping the unqualified from doing so is an honorable job; it is regrettable that sometimes it requires harshness and cruelty.

Lawyers on both sides can be much more cruel to prospective jurors than our prosecutor was. They can be caustic, disparaging, insulting, abusive. But unless a lawyer is quick to anger, the chances are that he will employ offensive tactics quite deliberately and only after deciding that he is ready to resort to the peremptory challenge if he has to. Otherwise, he runs the risk of antagonizing someone who will eventually sit on the jury, an error that can have lethal consequences for him. The last thing a lawyer needs—and a relatively easy thing for him to prevent —is to be faced with a juror who is his enemy from the start.

At one recent trial the *voir dire* was lumbering toward the end of its third day. Nine jurors had been chosen, though over 100 had been interrogated. As the afternoon dragged on, the tempers of the judge, the defense attorney, and the prosecutor had been getting shorter and shorter. The defense attorney in particular had become angry, almost savage in his questioning of several people and once or twice had even had to be admonished by the judge. Finally, there were only six prospective jurors left in the courtroom. The judge decided to dispense with the roll of the drum and the drawing of names. After telling all six to rise, he wearily asked if they had heard the instructions he had given to those previously summoned to the jury box. The six nodded. They had been in the courtroom since ten in the morning, and they had heard the lecture many, many times.

"Fine," sighed the judge. "Then I won't have to repeat myself. Let me just ask you—and I mercifully hope that no one says yes: Do any of you feel you have a *legitimate* reason for not serving on this jury?"

One hand shot up immediately, so swiftly it was as if it had been released by a spring. The owner of the hand, a man, shouted, "Yes, your honor, I do!"

The judge shook his head, impatient and disgusted. "What is it?" he asked. "And I'll tell you now, it had better be good."

The man stepped into the aisle. "Your honor," he began, "I have been so offended by the tactics I've witnessed in this courtroom today that I know I could not judge this case fairly." Now he was shouting again. "Defense counsel has treated people so barbarically that more than once I've wondered who's on trial here. I refuse to spend days listening to this . . . this shyster, and I am proud to admit to the court my absolute and total prejudice."

The man was not applauded but he was excused, and the defense eventually won the case.

ORDER
IN THE
COURT

*What the Court
Expects of a Juror*

You are one of the chosen, but for a long time your part, however demanding, will be passive and limited. Although your "tryout" required that you speak at some length, now in the courtroom you are expected to perform in silence, only to listen and to look. Furthermore, having been called to play a crucial role in the trial—sharing in the decision making that will determine its outcome—you may, ironically, hear and see considerably less of the proceedings than will a person who attends every trial session merely as a spectator.

As we begin our consideration of what happens during a criminal trial, we mention these paradoxes of jury service in order to emphasize that while the final verdict is the jury's, all other decisions of consequence are made by someone else, namely the presiding judge. After you have taken an oath—your first official act as a juror—and sworn that you will discharge your responsibility to the best of your ability, you are given a series of instructions by the judge that make dramatically clear his control over the events that follow.

His instructions are, in effect, the rules that are to govern the conduct of the jurors throughout the trial.

Discussing the Trial

Determined above all to preserve jury objectivity and open-mindedness, the judge does not want jurors to share their opinions, doubts, and observations with each other until the proper moment, and he does not want them to exchange views with husbands, wives, children, other relatives, or friends until the trial is over. Thus, the first judicial admonition in every trial— no matter the crime at issue and no matter the circumstances— is that jurors not discuss the matter at hand among themselves or with anyone else in any place and at any time. The judge will repeat this rule tirelessly, before every trial recess, before every lunch break, and at the end of every day of testimony.

Why this compulsive ban on talking about the very topic in which all the jurors have a common interest? The reason is almost self-evident. To a greater or lesser degree, we are all affected in our thinking by what we hear from others. Often we change our opinions of movies, books, and people after discussing them with someone whose intelligence we respect. And it is not only opinions that are susceptible to outside influence. Our perceptions—the way we see the world around us—can be altered, too, by someone who offers us information of which we were previously unaware or who suggests a perspective different from our own. An abstract painting that seems an ugly and meaningless jumble of forms, lines, and colors can suddenly convey purpose and emotion, and, hence, become beautiful when the techniques and the intent of the artist are explained to us.

Each juror is an individual, and, until that time when the twelve individuals must speak with one voice, it is the law's intention that each bring to the trial his or her *own* way of seeing and understanding and evaluating the people and the evidence presented. In most criminal trials twelve jurors are required—not three, not seven, not ten—because, among other reasons, it is believed that the greater the number of people exercising their unique powers of perception and judgment, the greater the chances of a fair trial.

Imagine a trial where, let's say, the third juror has a commanding personality and speaks more articulately, more authoritatively—and just plain louder—than any of her eleven colleagues. In the jury room, during a recess, this woman, in disregard of the judge's instructions, is holding forth on the defendant's "shifty eyes, drumming fingers, and tapping feet." Quite the astute observer, she declares, "Every minute something else starts moving. Did you notice? The fellow is a perpetual motion machine. Why is he so nervous if he's not guilty?"

Of course, a display of nervousness is not necessarily a sign of guilt; how, indeed, could a defendant not be tense when so much is at stake? Nonetheless, the third juror's observation will unquestionably infect the thinking of the others. Back in the courtroom after the recess, will there be even one among them who will not immediately focus on the fidgeting of the defendant? "By God, she's right," some will say. "Just look at those fingers go!"

It is bad enough for jurors to be influenced in this way by one of their own group, but it is much worse for them to be swayed by someone who is not even present at the trial. Our third juror was at least commenting on behavior that all the jurors could see and judge for themselves. Moreover, later, during the jury's deliberations, she will have the right and the responsibility to air her opinions and to try to persuade others to view things in her way. But for an outsider—for example, a man who comes no closer to the courthouse than the parking lot where he picks up his wife at the end of each day—to comment on a trial to a juror can be much more dangerous.

Again let's imagine a setting—the front seat of an automobile; a set of characters—a husband consumed with curiosity about the trial on which his wife, now by his side, is the sixth juror; a situation—they are driving home; and a dialogue:

Husband: Well, how did it go today?

Juror #6: All right, I guess.

Husband: What went on? Did that nightclub dancer testify?

Juror #6: She did, but I've told you before, I'm not supposed to talk about it.

Husband: Oh, come off it. You think the judge is hiding in the back seat? What did Lana Luverly have to say?

Juror #6: Not all that much, really. Some stuff about the defendant being very excitable and jealous. Honestly, Joe, I don't want to go into detail. I'll tell you everything when the trial is over, I promise.

Husband: By then you won't remember, and the guys down at the plant won't care any more. One of them was telling me today that he used to date Lana Luverly, in the days when she was Lillian Pugh. He said you can't believe a word she says. She'll lie if you ask her the time of day. If I was on that jury I'd

listen to her and believe just the opposite of what she testifies.

Juror #6: She sounded very convincing to me.

Husband: Of course she's gonna sound convincing. Her heart is in her work. Everyone knows she's dead set on getting rid of a boyfriend. It's been obvious she's helping to frame him ever since the poor shnook was arrested.

Now the sixth juror, simply by listening to her husband's remarks—remarks based on a prejudgment that, incidentally, would have kept him off the jury had *he* been called to serve—risks being influenced by them. She has, in a sense, been exposed to a disease. Of course, she may not catch it, but it is in the court's best interest to eliminate all the sources of infection. And so we have that incessant judicial admonition: do not talk about this case with anyone.

Actually, our curious husband was committing a crime. No doubt it will go unreported—and, therefore, unprosecuted—but he was guilty of the offense of *jury tampering.* Only people with official standing in the courtroom are permitted to try to influence the jurors. All others are prohibited from doing so. It is rare but not unknown for jurors to be threatened or to be offered bribes. But even far less blatant attempts to "get to" a juror would, if brought to the court's attention, be grounds for arrest. At the slightest hint of jury tampering, judges will often declare a mistrial—that is, terminate the trial at whatever point it has reached, dismiss all the jurors, and begin all over again. Needless to say, this is a drastic and costly action, but it is a necessary one given the circumstances. For the court, preserving the integrity of the jury is a matter of obsessive concern. For each individual juror it should be no less.

In reality, jurors do on occasion discuss the trial, among themselves and with others. Whether they allow themselves to be influenced by these conversations is another matter. As a juror, your thinking may be affected so subtly by a chance remark that you will not even be aware of it. And *that* is the danger. Just as the law dictates that the judge must be in control of the presentation of evidence, the law insists that you be in command of your reception of the evidence. Every time you talk of the trial you run the risk of losing command, of giving to others, who in the eyes of the law are less qualified to judge, some of the power that should be yours alone.

The integrity of the jury is a matter of such deep concern that at no time during a trial should it even *look* as if a juror's impartiality is being compromised. And so the judge will instruct you to avoid all outside-the-courtroom contact with the principals in the case. If you meet the district attorney in the courthouse elevator, don't expect him to say hello and don't try to engage him in conversation about the weather. If at a large weekend party you spot the defense attorney among the guests, pretend you don't know him. You can be sure he will pretend that he doesn't know you. Strangers you are and strangers you must remain, at least until the trial is over.

Visiting the Scene of the Crime

The judge's next caution to the jury may seem more farfetched:
you will be warned not to visit the scene of the crime. While it
may seem unlikely that a juror would want to do this, in some
trials the temptation is strong and not a matter of idle curiosity.
Quite the contrary. It is the conscientious juror, the one who
wants to understand fully the details of a crime, who would be
most inclined "to play detective." The testimony offered by
witnesses seems incomplete, unclear, or unbelievable; it cries out
for verification. How brightly lit was the place where the crime
was committed? Was the foliage so thick that a person could
crouch behind it and expect not to be seen? Where exactly was

the so-called eyewitness standing in relation to the defendant? A juror might well think that a nighttime or weekend excursion to the crime site might dispel some doubts or clarify some points that are at issue. But, in the eyes of the law, the juror would be amiss in thinking so.

It is the judge alone who decides which evidence may be presented to the jury and how it may be presented. At the court's direction, juries are sometimes brought *en masse* to the scene of the crime, to see for themselves what cannot be adequately re-created for them in the courtroom. But for one or two or even all twelve of the jurors to make such a trip on their own denies to the judge control over an experience that may prove crucial to the final verdict.

The fact of the matter is that direct observation can actually be misleading and make the search for truth that much more difficult. For example, the physical circumstances of a crime can never be exactly duplicated. At 5 P.M. on a Saturday at the end of November, a street corner will look quite different from the way it did at 4 P.M. on a Wednesday in early May when a holdup was committed there. Jurors who trust their own direct observation much more than any statements offered to them in a courtroom must learn to accept the handicap the court imposes. Even if they don't agree with it, they disregard it at their peril. To illustrate:

In a recent sensational murder case in New York City, a jury's verdict of guilty was overturned on appeal and a new trial ordered simply because a group of jurors had decided "to see for themselves." One night during the trial, at approximately the same hour it was believed the murder had been committed, the jurors traveled to the scene of the crime. Since their nocturnal outing was not publicly known until after the trial was over, its effect on the jury's verdict was uncertain. But that it took place at all was basis enough for the appeal justices to cry foul and to set aside the guilty decision.

Sequestration

A judge's concerns may differ from case to case, and certain of his instructions are "special" in that they reflect the particular circumstances of the case being tried. For example, if there has been and continues to be intensive press coverage of the crime and its aftermath, the judge will prohibit the jurors from having any contact with reporters or interviewers. He may indeed *sequester* the jurors—that is, remove them from all possible outside influences by putting them up in a hotel for the duration of the trial, forbidding them all visitors, and censoring the newspapers they read, the radio programs they listen to, the television programs they watch.

Sequestration is talked about and written about so often that people tend to think that it happens to all or most jurors. The truth is that it happens to very few, usually to those who, depending on your point of view, are fortunate or unfortunate enough to be empaneled for highly publicized trials. Obviously, it is only such trials that demand sequestration (and, even then, there are many press-reported trials in which the jurors are permitted to return to their homes every night). But the overwhelming majority, probably more than 99 percent, of the criminal trials held in the United States during any given year, on charges ranging from shoplifting to murder, generate not a line of newspaper copy or a second of television news time.

Paying Attention

There is, finally, one other judicial instruction that is common to all trials. It is less a rule than a plea: jurors must listen as intently and absorb as thoroughly as their capabilities allow. While the hours in the jury box creep by, you are likely to be puzzled, confused, bored, fascinated, skeptical, moved, angry, impatient, disgusted—and, perhaps, several of these simultaneously. But, the judge declares, at all times you are to remain alert and attentive and to commit to memory as much of what you hear and see as you can. (Note taking, usually, is a luxury not permitted to jurors.) Your failure to do so can have sad consequences, as illustrated by this classic story of juror inattention.

The trial was for rape. The prosecution's chief witness was the victim, who identified the defendant as her attacker and admitted that she knew him well. Indeed, they worked in the same office. She claimed that sometime before the crime was committed, the defendant wrote her a note with an obscene suggestion. The prosecution produced the note; the handwriting was authenticated by an expert as that of the defendant, and the judge thereupon allowed the note to be entered into evidence. While it was being stamped with an identifying number, the judge warned the jurors that they might be offended by the language of the note, but, he assured them, it was vital that they read it.

Surprisingly, perhaps, given the sensational nature of the case, the tenth juror had fallen asleep before the note was mentioned in testimony. He continued to nap as the expert verified the handwriting, as the judge spoke to the jury, and of course as, in total and shocked silence, the scandalous note was passed from juror to juror. Juror #9 was a woman. She was aware of the comatose state of the gentleman to her left, and she dreaded having to wake him. But she had no choice, for otherwise he would never take the note from her. So, after reading it herself, she poked him gently and inconspicuously in the arm with her elbow. He awoke immediately, slightly flustered, and, with a start, accepted the note she handed to him. He read it, blushed crimson, stole a quick glance at his neighbor to the right, and fumbled for his pen. Before he could scribble a reply, the judge asked him to please pass the note to the next juror.

PIECES
OF A
PUZZLE

What Jurors
May Expect
from a Trial

As in any game, after the referee has laid down the rules, the contest begins. So, having heard what the court expects from them (and from the attorneys, for the judge may have instructions for them as well), the jurors are now confronted with their first challenge: absorbing and understanding the attorneys' opening statements.

In the world outside the courtroom these statements would be labeled "propaganda"—information or ideas designed to promote or to damage a cause. (The classic example of propaganda in literature is Mark Antony's address to the Roman populace in Shakespeare's *Julius Caesar.*) Each of the opening statements will set forth conflicting arguments—the defense, assuming it makes an opening statement, will assert the innocence of the defendant, the prosecutor the guilt—but neither side will yet support its argument with proof of any kind. Each is hoping to persuade by the singular power of well-chosen words.

Their speeches will be bursting with sentences that begin, "We will show. . . ." "We will prove. . . ." "We will demonstrate. . . ." But remember that propaganda is not necessarily in the interest of truth, and since in most trials the defendant is either guilty or innocent (there are, of course, those cases where a plea of not guilty is based on a claim of insanity or self-defense rather than a denial that the defendant performed the criminal act), sheer logic tells us that the two opening statements cannot be equally valid. However, at this point it will be impossible for any open-minded juror to determine which of the attorneys is on the side of the angels. You shouldn't even try. There will be time enough for this after you have heard the evidence. What you can grasp is the shape of the case each side is to argue—the *kinds* of evidence each will present, and the way each will put the pieces of evidence together to form a whole. Understanding this overall design will later help you to follow the evidence as it is offered.

Following the evidence—the jurors' most essential and demanding task. Ideally, it is the evidence that will serve as the "great persuader" of the jury, evidence in the form of testimony by witnesses and the witnesses themselves—the way they talk, the way they look, the way they act—reinforced, perhaps, by certain physical objects.

In reality, of course, it is sometimes the eloquence, shrewdness, or showmanship of one attorney or the other that wins the case. But even in trials where a lawyer's skill is the deciding factor, the witnesses usually act as the instruments on which he displays his talent.

The prosecution presents its case first. Normally, it begins by calling to the stand witnesses who testify to the fact that a crime was committed and, in a murder trial, who establish the identity of the victim (or victims). They are followed by witnesses who describe how the crime was committed. These same witnesses or those who come after them then reach to the heart of the matter —the ways in which the defendant was supposedly involved in the crime and, finally, the proof or the powerful suggestion that he was actually responsible for the offense with which he is charged.

Inadmissible Evidence

At any point during this parade of witnesses, the defense attorney can object—either to a question asked or to an answer given. The judge then rules on whether the objection is valid. If he decides that it is not, he announces, "Objection overruled," and the witness may proceed with his answer or the prosecutor may go on to his next question. Should the judge decide that the objection is valid, he declares, "Objection sustained." If a question was at issue, the prosecutor must drop it entirely or rephrase it in an unoffending way. If a witness's answer prompted the objection, jurors face a strange challenge, for the judge will then instruct them to disregard the witness's last statement. How preposterous!

You never for a moment considered visiting the alleyway where the crime was committed. You didn't much mind having to ignore the defense attorney and his client as they had lunch two tables away from you in the Italian restaurant across the street from the courthouse. You resisted the temptation to tell a friend about the model who yesterday testified to owning nineteen fur coats. You even managed to keep your mouth shut when, in the jury room, the ninth juror complained that he didn't understand what the D.A. was driving at this morning. But, now, to be ordered to disregard a crucial bit of testimony, to pretend that the words have not been said. . . . Can the judge be serious?

He can be and he is. All that he is demanding, however, is that the offending statement have no effect on your judgment about the guilt of the accused. He is not requiring the impossible—that you forget what you heard or that you delude yourself into thinking you didn't hear it. He is merely trying to prevent you from being influenced by statements that the law considers unworthy of consideration.

During the course of the trial both sides are likely to register a fair number of successful challenges. Some of the more common grounds for challenge include:

• *Hearsay evidence*—testimony given by a witness based on what he has heard from another person rather than what he has seen or experienced directly. Example:

Question: What time did the defendant arrive at the country club that night?

Answer: I didn't see him until after midnight but someone told me he was there by ten.

• *Irrelevant and immaterial evidence*—testimony that misses or goes beyond the point at issue and/or the question that has been asked. Example:

Question: What was the defendant wearing?

Answer: Just a shirt and an old pair of blue jeans, but I know he has a closetful of expensive clothes and drives around in a Cadillac.

• *Statement of opinion*—testimony that expresses what a witness *thinks* rather than what he or she *knows* or has *experienced*. Example:

Question: Did the defendant finally pay the check?

Answer: Well, from the way he was talking about how the staff there all knew him and the headwaiter was his brother-in-law and other stuff like that . . . To be honest, I was in the kitchen when he left, but I would certainly *doubt* that he paid.

All three responses are clearly inadmissible as evidence. The chances are that when the judge directs you, as a juror, to disregard such statements, you will understand his reasons for doing so. Will that make it easier to obey him? Not necessarily. But if they do stick in your mind you should make a conscious effort not to let them lead you to conclusions that are otherwise unsupported. Like outside influences, inadmissible evidence confuses the matter at hand. Concern yourself only with admissible testimony and you will find your job as a juror arduous enough.

Physical Evidence

There are so many different kinds of admissible evidence, in categories broad and narrow, that during any one criminal trial you are not likely to encounter them all. The most general division is between physical evidence and oral testimony. The former encompasses everything from threads found lodged in a victim's fingernails to panoramic photographs taken of a crime site. It includes all sorts of:

• *Documents*—most notably, police and medical examiner reports, including fingerprints and ballistic tests, and transcripts of statements made prior to the trial, but also letters, bills, canceled checks, and every other type of written or printed material imaginable.

• *Objects*—weapons, clothing, automobile parts, jewelry, and other loot in all forms, shapes, and sizes.
• *Copies or reproductions of material that could not otherwise be shown in the courtroom*—blueprints, diagrams, and artist's sketches, plaster casts of footprints or tire tracks, recordings, videotapes and, of course, photographs of diverse people, places, and things.

Physical evidence is as subject to challenge as oral testimony, often on the grounds of its authenticity or because of the manner in which it was obtained. How can anyone be sure that the evidence is exactly what the defense or prosecution claims it to be? Couldn't that incriminating letter be a forgery? Did the police have a search warrant when they found the defendant's muddy boots in the cellar of his home? Of course, those become matters for the judge to decide. Indeed, whether challenged or not, physical evidence cannot be presented without the judge's specific approval. Once he has ruled an item admissible, it is given an identifying marking (Prosecution Exhibit A, B, C, etc., Defense Exhibit 1, 2, 3, etc.) and turned over to the jury for examination.

Jurors tend to appreciate physical evidence. It seems so much more reliable than oral testimony. Everyone knows that, intentionally or not, people lie, misspeak, forget, misinterpret, misunderstand. Physical evidence, when it has been properly authenticated, is solid and unchanging. If ballistic tests prove that the gun, Exhibit A, was the murder weapon, and if the gun carried fingerprints, Exhibit B, that match those of the defendant, Exhibit C, the jury may feel well, and happily, along the way to a guilty verdict. Physical evidence seems so reassuring, totally objective, and incontrovertible.

The only trouble is that often it is none of those things. While physical evidence, except for recordings, cannot speak, human voices can speak about it. And once they do, that welcome feeling of certainty may, abruptly or gradually, vanish into the air. Thus, defense counsel may acknowledge that Exhibit A was indeed the murder weapon and that it bore the defendant's fingerprints. He admits that his client held the gun, but denies that he shot it. In the face of damning physical evidence, he calls to the stand three witnesses who testify that they saw the defendant draw the gun from its holster, grasp it in a trembling hand, and then drop it and run. The jurors are thus wrenched from that secure little corner they briefly inhabited and thrust back into the world we all know, where people talk a lot but not always intelligibly and not always believably.

Eyewitnesses

Perhaps, the most troublesome kind of oral testimony is that of so-called eyewitnesses. These are people who supposedly were "there"—"there" being the scene of the crime at or near the time of its occurrence. One might think that an eyewitness would be the most effective type of witness, and, to be sure, prosecutors have been known to press upon juries such claims as, "While I cannot furnish you with movie film or videotape of the defendant in the act of committing the crime, I offer you the *next best thing* —eyewitness testimony." In truth, prosecutors, along with defense attorneys, judges, and jurors, know that eyewitnesses are often unreliable, implausible, and dangerous.

Experiments have proved that fifteen intelligent, clearsighted people can view the very same event and come up with fifteen different versions of it. Under the best of circumstances, our powers of observation are faulty and incomplete. The fact is that most crimes are crisis situations even for innocent bystanders; they evoke shock, bewilderment, fear, and perhaps terror, all of which tend to cloud and distort a witness's vision. To make matters worse, eyewitness testimony is based not only on observation but on memory, since the crime has always occurred long before the witness takes the stand.

An eyewitness will of course be questioned gently by the attorney for whom he is testifying, and, to the greatest extent possible, he will be allowed to tell his story in his own way. The opposing attorney will, however, substitute knives for kid gloves —scraping, piercing, probing the fabric of the testimony, he will try to reduce it to shreds, and very often he will succeed. He may compare the eyewitness's courtroom testimony with statements made to the police or the district attorney long before the trial began—that is, much closer to the date of the crime. He may contrast it to the testimony of other eyewitnesses. He may dig into areas that the witness tried to avoid in his original testimony because he didn't remember them very well. In short, the attorney will try to uncover enough inconsistencies, contradictions, gaps, and improbabilities to render the eyewitness's testimony worthless in the minds of the jurors.

He may go even further and suggest that the eyewitness is not simply an innocent, neutral bystander, but that he has a reason for lying—antipathy for the defendant, a desire for revenge, the promise of a reward if the defendant is convicted, the hope of leniency from the D.A.'s office in prosecuting charges the witness himself faces, or even the granting of immunity from those charges. If successful, the opposing attorney can so severely diminish the credibility of the witness, not only in what he has said but in *why he has said it,* that the juror is left not with the next best thing to videotape but with a puzzle that has no solution.

Witnesses for the Defense

Eyewitnesses are more often called by the prosecution than by the defense. Two other types of witnesses, *character witnesses* and *alibi witnesses,* appear only for the defense.

Character witnesses testify for but one purpose: to convince the jury that the accused is a fine and upright person—considerate, loving, generous, brave, hardworking—take your choice of favorable adjectives. Should a character witness speak something less than the truth, he makes himself particularly vulnerable to the prosecution's attack. If he has said that the defendant was a good student, expect the prosecutor to know, and to ask why, the defendant was expelled from high school. If the character witness has testified to the defendant's deep devotion to her children, depend on the prosecutor to know, and to ask why, they are being brought up by their grandmother.

The testimony of an alibi witness will relate more directly to the matter at issue. Its intent is to convince the jury that the defendant was somewhere other than the scene of the crime when the criminal act was committed.

Alibi witnesses are likely to be subjected to cross-examination that is a good deal sharper and more aggressive than that faced by character witnesses. As long as we all believe that a person cannot be in two places at the same time, the prosecutor knows that a truly persuasive alibi witness spells disaster for his case. The D.A. is in especially deep trouble if the alibi witness is a stranger to the defendant but, fortunately for the state, most alibi witnesses are friends or relatives and thus their credibility is immediately suspect. To press this advantage, the prosecutor will probably concentrate on the relationship between alibi witness and defendant, rather than on the alibi itself. If the defendant's mother or wife or girl friend testifies that he was with her watching television at the moment the crime was committed, the prosecutor may routinely ask, "What program was on?" "What time did it begin?" "What time was it over?" But far more crucial to the impact of his cross-examination will be such questions as, "You love your son very much, don't you?" or, "You wouldn't like to see your husband go to prison, would you?" or, "The defendant has promised to marry you, hasn't he?" By stressing the obvious—that these alibi witnesses have a powerful reason for lying—the prosecutor tries to drain their testimony of its usefulness to the defense. The alibi fades into insignificance; it becomes a story the jury should disregard, nothing more than a desperate but futile attempt to protect a loved one from the punishment he deserves.

The Defendant as Witness

There is one type of alibi witness who is unique in his potential to move the jury—the defendant himself. The Fifth Amendment of the Constitution guarantees that no person "shall be compelled in any criminal case to be a witness against himself." The right to avoid self-incrimination translates into the defense counsel's constant reminder to the jury, during the *voir dire* and afterward, that the accused need not take the stand in his own defense. Moreover, the defense attorney will insist, his client's failure to testify must not in the jury's mind create any implication of guilt. But like the judge's instructions to overlook a challenged piece of testimony, the protection against self-incrimination is something that jurors may find difficult to accept. While they may say they understand and believe in it, faced with the confused and ambiguous realities of a trial, they may almost unconsciously reject it. If a juror, after listening carefully to all the testimony and examining all the physical evidence, remains uncertain of what the verdict should be, or is no more than inclined to a judgment of guilt or innocence, such a juror may silently demand that the defendant take the witness stand. For only the accused, the juror thinks, speaking out loud and clearly in the courtroom can supply the necessary missing element.

From the point of view of the defense attorney, however, a defendant as witness is a doubled-edged sword, and sometimes one edge can be a great deal sharper than the other. For one thing, the defendant may prove to be a poor witness in his own behalf, even on direct examination. We must make a distinction here between what he says and how he is likely to appear to the jury. If his alibi is weak or nonexistent, it is usually pointless for him to take the stand. What can he possibly say to lead the jury to believe he is innocent? But even if he has an alibi that is reasonably credible, his lawyer must worry about the impression he will make on the jury. If he'll walk with a swagger as he crosses from the defense table to the witness stand, if he's likely to be surly and arrogant or to appear excessively nervous and uncomfortable (remember those shifty eyes, drumming fingers, tapping feet), if his answers are going to seem hesitant and tentative rather than forthright, he may indeed be better off sitting silently at the defense table, letting others do battle for him.

Even more compelling is the second reason for keeping defendants out of the witness box: once they have entered it voluntarily, they expose themselves to the most vigorous assault the state can muster. While the Fifth Amendment precludes the prosecution from calling a defendant to the stand, it in no way limits the state's prerogative to cross-examine an accused person who freely chooses to testify. Such a person is protected only by his attorney's right to object to any given question the prosecution may pose. Thus you, as a juror, are likely to hear during

cross-examination of the defendant more objections from the defense counsel, more vehemently voiced, than at any other time during the trial. But an objection made is not necessarily an objection sustained, and a defendant in the witness box is as vulnerable to injury as a soldier walking through a minefield.

If there are any weaknesses in his alibi, you can be sure the prosecutor will spot them, enlarge them, and probe them in an onslaught of questioning that is designed to demolish the alibi entirely. If the alibi is strong, the prosecutor can direct his fire at the defendant's hostile relationship to the victim or his ownership of a weapon or his sudden attempt to leave town or any other past action that can be made to seem suspect. Or the prosecutor may take as his target the very personality and character of the defendant. Using intimidation and antagonism as his weapons, he will try to goad the witness into a burst of temper that will offend the jury or, better yet, into an unthinking, damning admission. Caught off guard, the defendant may, with a single statement, subvert the defense that he and his attorney have labored diligently to build.

Finally and—in many cases—most important, the prosecutor may ask the defendant about his criminal record. By law, the state may not allude to a defendant's previous arrests and convictions if the accused does not take the stand. But if he does, his past immediately becomes permissible ground for questioning, and, should it be pitted with violations of the law, it becomes a particularly fertile one for the prosecutor. The revelation of a criminal record is, obviously, one of the most damaging kinds of evidence that can be presented to a jury.

Whenever a defendant takes the stand, the jury feels a special sense of expectation, one that no other witness can possibly arouse. Now you will hear directly from someone—maybe the only person in the world—who, without any qualification, knows the truth. Sad to say, the expectation, however thrilling, often remains unsatisfied. The defendant testifies and testifies and testifies, but after he has returned to his seat at the defense table, the jurors may be as uncertain as they were before he answered his first question. For while the defendant as a person may be unique in his absolute knowledge of his own guilt or innocence, as a witness he may be no more nor less convincing than any eyewitness or character witness or alibi witness. The jury craves the truth, but there is no assurance that the defendant, protesting his innocence, will offer it to them.

Direct and Circumstantial Evidence

What appears to be the truth may come from evidence of a type we have not yet considered. The testimony of eyewitnesses who claim to have seen the crime being committed, of character witnesses, of alibi witnesses, of the defendant himself are all categorized as *direct evidence*—statements that if factual, as they purport to be (they may, of course, be false), would, in and of themselves, prove the accused to be innocent or guilty. "I saw the defendant kill the man." "The defendant was sitting next to me at the movies at the time of the robbery." "I've known the defendant for fifteen years, and he's never been in the slightest trouble or done anything wrong." "I didn't do it." Such statements may or may not be believed by the jurors, but acceptance or rejection is all they require.

Another kind of evidence, however, demands more: statements or items of physical evidence that taken by themselves do not *prove* anything but that *suggest* certain conclusions are called *circumstantial evidence.* Presented with such evidence, jurors may believe or disbelieve it, as the case may be; but if they believe it, they are expected to take one additional step and reach a determination that the evidence itself does not actually demonstrate. Here are some examples:

—An accountant takes out a $100,000 life insurance policy on his wife. Three weeks later they are mountain climbing and, the man subsequently claims, his wife stumbles and falls to her death. A month after that he is remarried, to a woman he had met shortly before he took out the insurance policy, and the newlyweds attempt to emigrate to Switzerland.

—Anne Gibbs discovers that her mink coat is missing from her closet and reports its theft to the police. Months later she is dining out and sees a woman who looks vaguely familiar enter the restaurant wearing a coat that is identical to the one that was stolen. Ms. Gibbs stares at the woman and suddenly remembers meeting her before. She had called at the Gibbs' house soliciting funds for a charity. The woman, now seated, has draped the coat over the back of her chair. Ms. Gibbs gets up, walks over to the woman's table and sees the initials "A.G." embroidered in the lining of the coat.

—Two musicians in a combo get into a violent argument during a break in their nightclub act. Several patrons hear the drummer say to the guitarist, "Just watch out, you creep. I'm going to get you yet," then see him leave by a side exit. Later, after the now drummerless combo has completed its last performance of the evening, the guitarist is jumped from behind as he walks to his car. He struggles, manages to rip a button from his assailant's jacket, and is finally stabbed in the shoulder. While he says he could not see who attacked him, he identifies the button as coming from the style of jacket that all members of the combo wear.

If you think the accountant is guilty of murder, the fund raiser guilty of grand larceny, and the drummer guilty of assault, you have been influenced by circumstantial evidence. There is no clear proof that any of these three committed the crimes suggested. But the facts of the cases as given here so strongly indicate their guilt that if the three were to be put on trial *and their juries were to hear no other evidence,* the prosecution would probably have three easy victories. Such is the power of circumstantial evidence.

But suppose that at a trial the accountant's defense attorney calls to the witness stand the defendant's son, who testifies that his father has given him the entire $100,000 in insurance money, and two friends of the victim, who testify that they heard the defendant plead with his wife not to go mountain climbing because, as was generally known, she tended to be clumsy and impulsive.

And suppose that the fund raiser's lawyer offers as evidence her call records, which show that she visited Ann Gibbs *after* the mink coat had been reported stolen, and a receipt for her coat, which proves that it was purchased at a thrift shop.

And suppose that the drummer's defense counsel produces as a witness a cab driver who testifies that early in the evening of the crime he picked up the defendant in front of the nightclub and drove him to a hotel on the other side of town, a distance so great that it would have been extremely difficult, though not impossible, for him to return to the crime scene by the time of the attack. What if he then follows this witness with the housekeeper of the hotel where the combo was staying and she testifies that the day after the assault the *bass player* asked her to replace a button on his jacket?

If you are no longer so certain that the three defendants are guilty, you have again been influenced by circumstantial evidence. For if we admit the possibility that the fund raiser's documents could have been falsified, which the prosecution is sure to try to establish, the circumstantial evidence offered in rebuttal *proves* nothing. It merely calls into serious doubt what the opposing side seemed to have demonstrated.

And so the jury, absorbing these conflicting items of evidence, is working a giant jigsaw puzzle in which the pieces do not seem to fit, or are too few, or too many. Eventually, the jurors will have to put together what they have, perhaps jamming some pieces in where they may not belong, discarding others that appear not to be part of the puzzle, and leaving holes for pieces they were never given. Actually, completing the puzzle—that is, reaching a verdict—is often not as difficult as this chapter suggests. Our purpose here is merely to show how serious a challenge a juror may face. Be prepared for the most confusing and the most complex jumble of evidence because occasionally even an open-and-shut case is suddenly, unexpectedly, open again.

Trial Interruptions

It is also best to be prepared for what may well be the most frustrating aspect of a juror's service: waiting, waiting again, and waiting yet again in that second home, the jury room. Once a trial has begun, you will be fortunate indeed if you are permitted to hear the testimony with interruptions only for lunch breaks and other occasional recesses. All too often the procession of witnesses or the questioning of a particular witness will be brought to an abrupt halt. One attorney raises an objection, the other counters it, both converge on the bench, they exchange whispered words with the judge, and the latter orders the jury out of the courtroom. Off you go to the jury room, there to wait for as long as it takes the judge to hear arguments on both sides of the dispute and to make a ruling.

The matter at issue may, for example, be a confession that the defense counsel wants to suppress. If, after hearing arguments from both sides, the judge agrees, the confession will obviously not be introduced as evidence. But if the jury were to be made aware merely that the confession exists, it is likely they would be influenced by that fact. Thus, the judge will not permit the jurors to hear about evidence that he may later rule inadmissible. If he should decide that it is admissible, they will learn about it soon enough.

(Incidentally, if a trial is given press coverage, banishing the jury while courtroom proceedings continue results in one of the paradoxes we spoke of earlier: people who read about the trial in the newspapers learn more about it than do the members of the jury.)

Legal disagreements relating to the presentation of evidence are only one of the reasons jurors must spend as much time as they do in the jury room. You may be told to report to court by

9:30 in the morning and then, finally, take your seat in the jury box at 11:00. Why? One of the lawyers overslept, or the judge is detained in dealing with other matters on his calendar, or the next witness scheduled to testify does not show up, or the opposing attorneys are negotiating the possibility of the defendant's changing his plea from not guilty to guilty of a lesser offense. The frustration that jurors feel as they read their books and newspapers, knit their sweaters, solve their crossword puzzles, and play their card games mounts as the minutes tick by. Like passengers on a train stalled between stations, they are usually given no reason for the delay. The reason, if they knew it, might prejudice them; not knowing it, their anger is evenly directed against both sides.

That anger has been known to have surprising consequences. In a burglary trial not too long ago, the weakness of the defense case was matched and masked by the bluster of the defense attorney. Again and again he jumped to his feet to shout objections and to demand consultations with judge and prosecutor. Because of him, seven times in the course of a day and a half the exasperated jurors were driven from jury box to jury room. The seventh time the wait seemed endless. Suddenly a woman juror lost her composure, stood up, and banged her chair violently on the floor.

A few minutes later the jury was ushered back into the courtroom to be told that the trial was over—the defendant had changed his plea—and to be thanked for their cooperation and their patience. They were free to go home.

They filed out of the courtroom, relieved but also dissatisfied. Their days of jury service now seemed so pointless, so wasteful. Then the prosecutor, smiling broadly, approached them. "Well, which one of you did it? Which one of you cracked the case?"

The jurors stared at him in silence.

"Come on, now," he went on. "One of you got mad and threw something on the floor, something heavy."

The culprit spoke up timidly. "I did," she said. "I just couldn't take that waiting anymore."

"Well, that broke it," the prosecutor said. "We were in the judge's chambers directly below the jury room and when Maguire [the defense attorney] heard that crash upstairs, he turned white. You scared the hell out of him. He figured he'd made you so angry by his delaying tactics that you'd wring a guilty verdict out of the jury if it killed you."

Now the woman smiled, too. "I think maybe he was right," she said.

WITH A LITTLE HELP FROM YOUR FRIENDS

The Attorneys' Summations

and the

Judge's Charge

to the Jury

You have heard and seen all the evidence. The prosecution has rested its case and so, in turn, has the defense. There is a good chance that you have already made up your mind. Your verdict may have been determined by a single witness who seemed to you so honest, so utterly convincing that all your doubts have been dispelled. Or the accumulation of evidence on one side or the other may be so massive that it leaves you with no room for reasonable doubt. In either case, if the prospect of deliberating seems no more attractive than a final exam or a visit to the dentist, it is only because you shrink from having to persuade others to think as you do or because you dread being pressured to change your own view.

But perhaps you are undecided, or merely *leaning* toward one verdict or the other. Deliberation looms as a mixed blessing. On the one hand, you feel, it may help you to clarify your thinking and to reach a firm decision; on the other hand, it may confuse you even more, creating doubts where none existed and leaving unanswered the questions that trouble you.

For the moment, at least, you can relax. Help of a sort is on the way. You will not be allowed to begin deliberation until the welter of evidence has been organized and put into perspective by three "servants" of the court—the defense attorney, the prosecutor, and the judge. True, when they have finished speaking, you may feel more bewildered than ever. But there is the strong possibility that you will learn from one of them or be swayed by another.

The Attorneys' Summations

The attorneys' summations together with their opening statements frame the picture that is the evidence. Since the two sides have presented very different evidence or have interpreted the same evidence in very different ways, the frames they use will, correspondingly, be of widely divergent styles. But they will be alike in one respect: they will enclose the picture within the most complementary settings the lawyers can devise. In other words, just as their opening statements were propagandist, so will their summations be. They will be trying to persuade you.

The defense summation may be first or it may follow that of the prosecution. Remember the lawyer in the case of the woman who wasn't there? His performance epitomized just how theatrical a closing statement can be. Many good defense attorneys are effective showmen. They try to play on the emotions of the jurors just as actors do with their audiences. It is of course unfair to generalize—many lawyers are methodical, low-key, and professorial. But for the defense often the very nature of the occasion —its last opportunity to save the defendant from a more or less severe penalty—seems to demand histrionics.

The defense summation tends to adhere to a set pattern. Let us assume that the defendant's case is not based on a plea of not guilty for reason of insanity or self-defense. Certainly in the overwhelming majority of criminal trials the accused's plea is a simple not guilty, without any qualifications. Counsel will probably begin by reminding the jurors that the burden of proof rests on the prosecution, that the state must prove the defendant guilty beyond a reasonable doubt. Since this may well be the defense attorney's strongest weapon, in his view he cannot use it too often.

He then proceeds to consider the state's case from a very special perspective. Using words that, like a fun house mirror, tend to distort, he will enlarge the weakest elements of the prosecution's evidence and diminish or ignore the strongest. If the testimony of a state's witness was contradictory or inconsistent, you can be sure that the flaws will now be pounced upon, poked at, and exhibited in all their incongruity. If a witness made statements that seemed implausible, the defense attorney will hold them up to ridicule. As he reviews all the evidence presented against his client, his manner will range from disparagement to mockery to anger. "How can the district attorney expect twelve sophisticated people to believe such illogical statements?" "A child in grade school could see through this transparent tissue of lies." "It is astonishing that the district attorney, presumably an honorable man of the law, would have you doom this young man to years in prison on accusations that are unsupported by a shred of real evidence. It is astonishing, it is shocking, it is shameless!" Denunciations such as these, the defense hopes, will jolt the jury into recognizing everything that is suspect in the state's case.

As for the defense's own evidence, the attorney may have none to review. You will recall that the lawyer for the husband of the woman who wasn't there called no witnesses at all. It is not unusual for the defense to summon few if any witnesses. There may be none to call, or the state's case may seem so weak that defense counsel will decide he can effectively demolish it in cross-examination of the prosecution witnesses and/or in summation. But you can be sure that if the defense did call witnesses who are presumed to have made a good impression on the jury, their testimony will now be remembered and quoted as if it were gospel. The weaknesses in that testimony will be overlooked, the strengths will be emphasized and repeated. As a juror you need not worry about forgetting some bit of evidence you heard days or weeks ago. Rest assured you will be reminded of it during the summations—by the defense attorney if it is favorable to his client, by the prosecutor if it is not.

Defense summations almost always end on an emotional note.

Even if an attorney has followed a matter-of-fact course in discussing the evidence, he is likely to conclude his summation with an earnest plea for compassion and mercy. If the defendant is a mother, you will be urged to remember the children who are waiting for her at home, and if the defendant is a teenager, you will be asked not to forget the mother who is longing for his return. If the defendant comes from a broken home or has led a life of poverty, you will be reminded of the suffering, the pain, and the deprivation he has already endured. If the defendant is a member of a minority group, you will be lectured on the discrimination and prejudice that society has inflicted on that group—if not specifically on the defendant himself. If the defendant is middle-class or wealthy and proof of some kind of wrongdoing (although not necessarily of the crime charged) is inescapable, you will be told that we all make mistakes and that to err is human, to forgive divine. In an era when poetry is little read and seldom quoted, defense summations are one of the last bastions of verse. Obviously, Shakespeare's "The quality of mercy is not strained . . ." is a favorite, but poems familiar and obscure droppeth as the gentle rain from the lips of lawyers. And if a defense attorney does quote poetry in his summation, you can be sure his delivery of it will be full-voiced and fervent—the actor in the lawyer will take center stage and stand revealed. Furthermore, if he has tears, be prepared: he will shed them now.

Prosecuting attorneys are just as likely to indulge a theatrical flair. But while defense attorneys can almost always run a gamut of emotions from fury (directed at those who are trying to convict their clients unjustly) to tenderness (directed at their clients), prosecutors, after expressing sympathy for the victim, usually limit themselves to the expression of a single feeling: outrage.

The D.A. has an important advantage over the defense attor-

CALDWELL

ney: he can attempt to rebut the points made by the latter in his summation without fear of counterrebuttal, for the prosecution has the last word. Depending on the court, the D.A. either follows the defense in his summation or, if he precedes it, is allowed to answer it with a rebuttal. For our purposes here, let us assume the prosecution's summation follows that of the defense. The D.A. will begin by denying or disputing everything of importance that you as a juror have just heard. And he will proceed—calmly, carefully, and conscientiously—to reassemble the building blocks of the state's case. He will review all the evidence that he has presented, or at least all that he now thinks useful. He will recall testimony in language that may carry more impact than the original statements of his witnesses. An eyewitness who seemed to you a trifle hesitant, as if not absolutely certain of what he saw, will be brought back to life as an unwavering accuser. A plaster cast of a footprint that was fluttery in its outline when you looked at it gains sharp definition when the district attorney describes it: now it is unquestionably a cast of the defendant's shoe. Compelled by the defense summation to consider the weaknesses in his case, the prosecutor will minimize them or try to dismiss them entirely. Inconsistencies in the testimony of one witness will be explained away by references to fear or the badgering of the defense attorney or imperfect memory. Contradictions between the testimony of two witnesses will be belittled by citing that famous experiment demonstrating that fifteen college students all observing the same incident later recalled fifteen differing versions of it. A witness who in the past has himself been in trouble with the law will now become for the prosecutor a model citizen whose only desire is that justice be done.

Almost all prosecution summations end in the same way: that sense of outrage that may earlier have found its target in the defense attorney is finally aimed at the defendant. From the mist of rhetoric he emerges as not merely the perpetrator of the crime with which he is charged, but also as a symbol of the collapse of law, order, and decency in the community today—a "menace to society." If the offense of which he is accused involves any kind of violence—arson, robbery, rape, assault, murder—the most brutal details and the most tragic consequences of the crime will be recalled in all their horror. Just as a defense attorney will appeal to the jurors' compassion, saying, in effect, "Even if you think my client is guilty, have pity on him because he has already suffered so much and let him go free," the prosecuting attorney will close by exploiting the jurors' fears, saying, in effect, "This defendant may well be one of the reasons you are scared to walk the streets at night." And if it is the defense's hope to leave you with your throat knotted and your eyes blinking away tears, it is the prosecution's intent to leave you shaken with anger that all around you innocent people are being victimized and fixed in your determination to root out one of the sources of danger.

Obviously, then, however effective either attorney may be in summation, they cannot be counted on to provide the sense of sobriety and reason that comes with an objective look at the matter at hand. Their aim is primarily to persuade, not to enlighten, and their methods often deliberately obscure and distort —rather than carefully analyze—the evidence that has been presented.

The Judge's Charge

Following the attorneys' summations, the judge delivers his closing message, the *charge to the jury.* It is regarded as the single most important statement made during a trial, and in many states, while he delivers it no one is allowed to enter or leave the courtroom.

Some states allow judges to review thoroughly all the evidence that has been offered to the jury. Witness by witness, they are free to summarize the testimony presented. This can be enormously useful to jurors, particularly if the trial has been long and the evidence complex. But it carries its own potential hazards, and this is why many states severely restrict the content of the judge's charge.

If after hearing all the evidence you, as a juror, have made up your mind as to the defendant's guilt or innocence, it is likely that the judge has done the same. Indeed, if the judge has concluded that the verdict must be not guilty because of the evidence (or the lack of it), he may actually halt the trial at this point and either dismiss all the charges or impose on the jury what is known as a *directed verdict* of acquittal. A directed verdict can never be a guilty verdict: the jury alone must reach that decision. But if the judge finds that the state's case does not clearly prove a violation of the law, he has the power to grant the defendant immediate freedom. The jurors in such a situation have performed their labors of looking and listening for no purpose—except that their presence was required for the prosecution's case to be exposed in all its inadequacy.

Only infrequently, however, does a judge abort a jury trial in this way. If he has merely come to an *opinion* as to the defendant's innocence or guilt, he must keep that opinion to himself. But, for some observers, therein lies the problem with having the judge summarize the evidence. It is exceedingly difficult, they say, for a judge to reconstruct for the jury all that has been disclosed during a trial without coloring his account with his own views.

If he believes the defendant guilty, he will, perhaps unintentionally, emphasize the most damaging testimony the prosecution was able to produce. If he believes the defendant innocent, he will, perhaps, give extended consideration to the witnesses for the defense. Try telling someone the plot of a movie you have seen without divulging what you thought of the picture. You will find that complete objectivity is almost impossible to achieve; the person hearing your version of the story will somehow sense your opinion. In much the same way a jury, listening intently to the judge's charge, can often detect in the words he chooses certain clues and implications that suggest the conclusion he has reached. This may be true for even the most discreet and responsible judge.

Some states permit the judge not only to summarize but also to comment upon the testimony, while others entirely prohibit this. More often comment is at the judge's discretion. To whatever extent it is allowed, it will, quite obviously, have its effect on the independent thinking of a jury. Imagine the impact of such judicial comments as these (all purely fictional and, deliberately, rather extreme):

"I call to your special attention the fact that the witness who tried so terribly hard to provide the defendant with an alibi is not only his brother but recently completed a five-year prison term for armed robbery."

"I want to remind you that while the defendant claims to have been playing basketball in the schoolyard at the time of the burglary, he could not come up with the name of a single person —not one—who was with him in the game."

"Bear in mind that on the night of the shooting it was raining torrentially, the streetlight was out—in fact, it wasn't repaired, we heard, until two days later—and the defendant we were told was running—in fact, racing—down the block. Ask yourself how reliable an identification a so-called eyewitness can make under such circumstances."

"Remember that the victim's checkbook was lying unattended on the top of her desk in an unlocked office for four hours and that samples of her signature were easily available to literally hundreds of her co-workers. She was, you might say, just about issuing an invitation to forgery—and issuing it to many more people than the defendant."

The context in which these comments were made could, of course, modify the effect they would have on the jurors' thinking. But taken out of context, can there be any question that the first two would hasten the respective defendants on their way to conviction and that the last two might be their tickets to freedom? In fact, the first two are so highly prejudicial that they could provide grounds for appeal; if a higher court agreed that the judge spoke improperly, it could then set aside a guilty verdict and order a new trial.

Of course, many will argue that the guidance a judge offers to a jury is to be welcomed rather than avoided. The advantages in giving direction to the thinking of a group of twelve confused and ordinary people far outweigh the risks, it is claimed; as we have seen, there are countries in which guidance is not merely permitted—it is required. But here in the United States a cornerstone of the jury system is the principle that, though a judge may be empowered to make observations about the trial evidence, jurors, once they are called upon to deliberate, must never surrender or minimize their own capacity for reaching judgments on what they have seen and heard. Our legal system has decreed that jurors have the final say regarding the truths of the case; in deciding upon the facts, you as a juror may not defer to anyone —neither the eleven other jurors nor the judge himself.

While there may be disagreement on the question of judicial commentary on evidence, no one can question the need for the other phase of the judge's charge to the jury—explanation of the indictment and instruction in the relevant law. If at the outset of a trial jurors are to be strangers to the law, before they begin their deliberations they had better be introduced. The introduction begins even before the *voir dire,* but for the most part it is contained in the judge's charge—the last statement the jurors hear before they retire to the jury room.

The judge will first read the counts of the indictment. If you are lucky there will only be one or two of them, but be prepared for eleven or fifteen or twenty-four. If the district attorney was able to convince the grand jury that the defendant probably broke many laws or that he *possibly* broke only a few, but the petit jury should ultimately decide which ones among many, you will be faced with a multicount indictment. Plainly, the greater the number of counts, the more complicated the case, the more decisions to be made, and, usually, the harder the jury must work to grasp the nature of the accusations against the defendant. The judge will carefully review each count of the indictment, explaining exactly which portion of the criminal code the defendant is charged with having violated and exactly what conclusions the jury must come to if it is to find the defendant guilty on that count. The judge will then inform the jury that they may find the defendant guilty on all counts, on most of them, on a few, on only one, or on none at all. To illustrate:

A young man is arrested for having shot his aunt, who suffered only a flesh wound. He is, however, charged with four counts:

1. attempted murder, which means acting with intent to kill;
2. assault in the first degree, which means inflicting *serious* bodily injury while intending to inflict *serious* bodily injury;
3. assault in the second degree, which means inflicting bodily injury while intending to inflict bodily injury (note the absence of "serious");
4. possession of an unlicensed gun, the meaning of which is self-evident.

In his charge to the jury the judge will fully explain the four counts of the indictment. But the crucial part of his instruction will be his definition of the *differences* among the counts and his setting forth of the conclusions the jury must unanimously arrive at in order to convict on any and all counts.

Thus the judge will advise the jurors that:

1. To find the defendant guilty of the first count, they must believe both that he quite deliberately shot his aunt (action) and that he wanted to kill her (intent). If they have reasonable doubt on one or both of these points, their verdict must be not guilty on the first count.

2. To find the defendant guilty of the second count, they must believe both that he quite deliberately shot his aunt (action) and that he wanted to injure her seriously (intent). Again absence of agreement on one or both of these points requires a not-guilty verdict.

3. To find the defendant guilty of the third count, they must believe both that he quite deliberately shot his aunt (action) but that he just wanted to hurt her a bit (intent). Once more, reasonable doubt on either or both of these points must result in a not-guilty verdict.

4. To find the defendant guilty of the fourth count, they must believe only that he had in his possession a gun he was not licensed to use. If they are not convinced he carried this gun, he must of course be found not guilty on the last count (and, practically and logically, must be innocent on all counts).

This model four-count indictment is a relatively simple one (which by no means implies that a jury will have an easy time reaching agreement about it). Indictments are often far more complex. It is not uncommon for a judge to spend a day or more in discussing a multicount indictment (although, conversely, this does not necessarily guarantee lengthy jury deliberations. Recently, in a month-long trial in New York City, a jury brought in a not-guilty verdict on a 192-count indictment after deliberating less than two hours!).

Finally, even more will be demanded of a judge's charge if the defense's plea is not guilty by reason of insanity or self-defense. We have mentioned such pleas earlier; they require the jury to make a determination quite different from whether or not the defendant committed the crime with which he is charged. Here the defense may acknowledge that he performed the act, but it argues that the offense is not punishable because either he was not responsible for his actions (that is, he was insane) or he was reacting to potential danger to himself or to others (that is, broadly speaking, he was acting in self-defense). Deciding whether there is merit in such a defense—particularly in the insanity defense, which is used in about 2 percent of criminal trials—can pose extraordinarily difficult problems for a jury. Experts disagree as to the very definition of the word "insane" in the context of a criminal trial. Does it mean the defendant was suffering from a mental disease or defect or does it mean he did not know what he was doing or does it mean he did not know that what he was doing was wrong? It is questions like these that the judge must answer in his charge to the jury. Required to explain the relevant legal doctrines in determining criminal responsibility, he will enter thickets entangled with issues of law, psychiatry, morality, and history. And the jurors must try to follow him every step of the way.

As a juror, perhaps nothing else that is expected of you will prove as challenging as listening to, concentrating on, and retaining all the facets of the judge's charge. In a complicated trial this can be a formidable task indeed, but in any trial it is an absolutely vital one. If you are to discharge your responsibility honorably and effectively, you must thoroughly understand the basis for the jury's deliberations: the precise crime(s) the defendant is alleged to have committed and the precise conclusions the evidence must demonstrate to support a verdict of guilty. No one except the judge can clarify these matters with objectivity and fairness. However long he speaks, however repetitious he may seem, however technical the language he uses, pay close attention to what he says. It is like a map offered to a traveler embarking on a journey. True, the map may suggest many routes to at least two destinations, but it's the only map there is.

ALONE AT LAST

*How Jurors Deliberate
and Reach Their Verdict*

Some juries never agree on a verdict at all. Their members spend hours and then days in reasoned discussion, angry debate, and desperate pleading. They exchange words, ideas, experiences, and invective. They admit their doubts, their prejudices, their fears—and, finally, their defeat. They are, it is said, "at an impasse" and "hopelessly deadlocked."

Agreeing only to disagree, they transmit this decision to the court, perhaps with reluctance, probably with disappointment, but mostly in exhaustion and relief. The judge—impatient, frustrated, irate—has no choice but to acknowledge their failure, particularly if he has refused to accept it earlier and again and again has sent them back to continue their deliberations. He is faced now with what is known as a hung jury. Quite possibly from his point of view and that of the prosecutor—though not necessarily that of the defense—the time, the effort, and the money spent on trying the case have been wasted. But if these twelve people could not reach a verdict perhaps another group of twelve can. And so the whole procedure may start again.

The forces that produce a hung jury are at work in every jury room—just as strong, just as active, and potentially just as divisive. But when they are brought under control, and they usually are—only 6 percent of all criminal trials end with a hung jury—the result, at least on the surface, is quite splendid: twelve people, thrown together by chance, have exercised their free will, their knowledge, and their intelligence to arrive unanimously at a crucial decision. Truly, we have here the ultimate expression of the democratic process.

Or do we? What actually happens in a jury room is usually neither as torturous as the struggle that ends in a hung jury nor as glorious as the ideal envisioned by those who gave us the jury system. The realities of jury behavior can be traced to nothing more or less than human nature; while, obviously, these realities are of vital interest to lawyers, political scientists, and even historians, they are equally the province of psychologists.

Since no "outsider" is ever allowed to observe or overhear what goes on in a jury room, studies of jury behavior are based for the most part on after-trial interviews with jurors, or on simulated juries made up of college students or of people challenged during a *voir dire*. Neither approach is totally satisfactory because neither can precisely reconstruct the way an actual jury functions: ex-jurors are not likely to recall everything they experienced of interest and importance, and simulated juries are free of that most burdensome responsibility of real juries, the knowledge that their verdicts will have serious consequences.

These weaknesses notwithstanding, studies of how juries deliberate are both fascinating and valuable and from them many generalizations can be drawn. Some of these will be dramatized later in five purely imaginary sketches of juries in action. But first let's describe where it all happens.

As you retire to deliberate, you return to the room where no doubt you have already spent a good deal of waiting time. It is a place of work, not of relaxation, and as such it is sparsely furnished and strictly functional. Dominated by a large table, it contains little else besides twelve reasonably comfortable chairs, some ashtrays, perhaps a water pitcher and glasses. If the room has windows—and it may not—don't expect a view or access to fresh air. The glass will be opaque or crisscrossed with steel mesh and the windows will be sealed and perhaps even barred. There will be no way for you to signal to anyone outside. And forget about leaving early. The door to the room is locked from the outside and can be opened only by the court officer who stands constant guard in the hallway. Once the jury has retired to deliberate, no one is allowed to enter or leave the jury room except under the most extraordinary circumstances (the sudden illness of a juror, for example), and the jurors may move only en masse to return to the courtroom or to go to a restaurant or hotel. There is a lavatory off the jury room—the only place where a juror can find solitude and the only place where two or three jurors can find a retreat from the rest of the group. In other words, the bathroom may, on occasion, be used for a purpose for which it was not designed.

Choosing a Leader

Once you are settled in the jury room, you may be eager or hesitant to begin deliberations, but in either case the forces that govern all group decision making—unstated, instinctive—immediately come into play; the first of these is the need for leadership.

In some states, like New York, the *nominal* leader is already known in that the first juror chosen in the *voir dire* is automatically the foreman or forewoman of the jury. Whether this person then becomes the *actual* leader of the deliberations depends upon several factors: his or her personality and experience in group leadership, the personalities of other members of the jury, and, if the nominal leader has already reached an opinion as to the defendant's guilt, how firmly he or she holds that view.

Certainly, the fact that a person has been designated foreman or forewoman and is acknowledged as such during the course of the trial provides him or her with a definite advantage in assuming real leadership. Once in the jury room, the eleven other jurors will expect that person to sit at the head of the table and will look to him or her to direct the initial discussion. This is a crucial moment in determining who will be the real leader of the deliberations and, perhaps, even in determining the jury's final verdict. Let us imagine three very different foremen and forewomen and their opening comments:

No. 1: "I've never served on a jury before and I don't know much about it, but I guess we should start by taking a vote."

No. 2: "If no one has any objection, I think we should go around the table so that each of us can say what he or she thinks."

No. 3: "Okay, so you should know where I stand, let me tell you that I think this joker is guilty from the word go. Now if anybody disagrees with me, let's hear it."

Foreman No. 1 is at best a reluctant leader. He begins by confessing his inadequacy and his first, rather tentative decision —to take a vote—actually serves to delay the time when he must assert himself. Beginning with a poll of the jurors, which is quite common in deliberations, provides among other benefits an immediate indication of the challenge ahead. After the outcome of the vote is known, Foreman No. 1 may decide that he can effectively take charge, but the chances are good that he will either deliberately relinquish his power to someone else or find his power gradually eroding as other more forceful jurors take command of the discussion. He will remain the only person through whom the other jurors, individually and collectively, may communicate with the court, and he will, of course, have the honor of publicly announcing the jury's verdict, but otherwise he will be no more than one of the group.

Forewoman No. 2 is a reasonable, thoughtful type—perhaps a natural leader, perhaps not. She rejects the easy choice of a quick vote in favor of an approach that will yield richer material for discussion and, at the same time, suggest the range of juror sentiment almost as clearly as polling will. It is unlikely that anyone will object to her around-the-table method although some jurors may elect to pass when it is their turn to speak. In any case, Forewoman No. 2 has demonstrated important leadership qualities in her opening statement. At this point, unless she is totally undecided about the verdict while most of the other jurors are in full agreement, she will probably be forewoman in more than name only.

Foreman No. 3, who may well have been a top sergeant in the army, is a "born leader." Perhaps not the best kind of leader for jury deliberations (or anything else), he is nonetheless a take-charge kind of person who immediately identifies himself as such, thereby challenging anyone to question his authority. Indeed, in his opening statement he is almost daring his fellow jurors to disagree with him. It is to be hoped that not everyone will be intimidated. But intimidation is one way of asserting leadership, and Foreman No. 3 uses it to try to solidify a position he originally attained purely by chance. He is foreman. Anybody want to make something out of it? Perhaps someone will.

Merely conferring the title of Foreman or Forewoman on someone does not then guarantee that that person will be the leader of the jury. In effect, the role must be earned by seizing control of circumstances. This can be true even when the foreman or forewoman is chosen by the more prevalent method of having the jurors select their own leader. If the jurors do not know one another very well—if the trial has been short or has moved very quickly—they have little or no basis on which to make a choice. Indeed, many juries finesse the issue by simply drawing lots. Obviously, a foreman chosen in this way is hardly more secure in his role than a first-juror foreman. The least vulnerable foreman is the person who wins the most votes in an election among those who feel they know him. Of course, the closer the balloting, the shakier his position. But, regardless of how the vote divides or how solid are the grounds on which the jurors make their choice, the election procedure automatically confers a legitimacy that a leader selected in any other way must work to—and may never—achieve.

The Deliberations Begin

With a leader in place, at least temporarily, the jurors begin their deliberations. Let's consider first a not-so-rare occurrence—reaching unanimity of opinion on the first go-around, be it by vote or organized discussion. Immediate and complete agreement among jurors happens more frequently than you might think—31 percent of the time, it is estimated. The jury in the Lizzie Borden trial was a dramatic illustration of the phenomenon—and for people who wish to avoid conflict and controversy and get home early, too—which probably means most of us—it is a cherished blessing. What brings it about?

Primarily, the weight of the state's evidence. There *are* open-and-shut cases, and more often they are shut on the guilty side: 19 percent of immediate verdicts are for conviction, 12 percent for acquittal. Moreover, when an effective attack by the prosecution is aimed at an unsympathetic defendant—someone who, whether he or she takes the stand or not, inspires suspicion, dislike, and distrust—you have a situation where twelve people can easily come to the same negative conclusion.

Conversely, a weak case by the prosecution can be further undermined by an attractive defendant—not merely physically attractive, although that certainly helps, but seemingly honest, clean-cut (which is why defense attorneys insist that their clients be well-groomed in the courtroom even if their normal mode of dress and hair style tends to the flamboyant), gentle, and—innocent. A quick not-guilty verdict may also be prompted by a flood of compassion for the defendant. Remember the defense summation in which the accused becomes the victim: "My client has suffered enough." When jurors can be made to see the defendant in an inordinately sympathetic light, and particularly when the crime with which he or she is charged is not regarded as terribly serious (shoplifting, for example) and the state's case is somewhat vulnerable, the chances are good that no one will vote for conviction. Acquittals like these almost always rest on the jurors' shared belief that, whatever the person may have done in the past, he or she is not likely to commit a crime in the future. Like Jesus in the *Book of John,* the jury is saying, "Neither do I condemn thee: go, and sin no more."

But it would be naive to enter a jury room expecting speedy agreement among a group of twelve very different individuals. Research has shown that even when jurors at the outset of their deliberations find themselves in substantial accord, they feel an obligation to discuss the case at some length. A jury that returns a verdict in less than an hour probably had no conflicts to resolve but enjoyed a thorough rehash of the trial.

Most juries, of course, do experience disagreement. Usually it emerges quite early and, at once, lines are drawn. People choose sides, leaving perhaps a pool of players, "the undecideds," who will later join one team or the other. But although the contest between the "guilties" and the "not-guilties" will take shape rather rapidly, it is difficult to know how long the game will last. However, if one side is much stronger in numbers than the other, it is fairly easy to predict the final outcome.

Common sense tells us that a division of votes that borders on unanimity—that is, eleven to one—means that the eleven are sure to triumph. In spite of such fictions as *Twelve Angry Men* (in which a single juror manages, after hours of dramatic confrontation, to twist and batter his colleagues around to his view), the position of a person who *from the beginning* stands apart as a lonely "holdout" is virtually insupportable. One of the fundamental rules of group behavior—and a rule that is so essential to the efficient discharge of a jury's duty that without it the very system probably could not exist—is that people want to identify with and be part of the majority.

It takes great personal courage and uncommonly strong conviction for anyone to hold to an unpopular view, and the degree of courage and conviction required is almost directly proportional to the unpopularity of that view. When it can be expressed as one against eleven, the pressure felt by the holdout—from the rest of the group and, more important, from within himself—will eventually become too painful to tolerate. The majority assumes that it is right if only because it *is* the majority, and a lopsided one at that; therefore, the odds against its losing power—that is, members—are staggering. Not only will the holdout be unable to win adherents to his side, he will eventually become the target of a relentless attack. From all around the table jurors will be urging him to remember certain pieces of evidence, reminding him of the testimony of one witness or another, demanding that he answer a variety of pointed questions, and—depending on how long it takes for him to succumb—begging him to be reasonable and assailing him for being pigheaded. Few of us could sustain such an onslaught for very long; almost inevitably the holdout will give in. Making his concession immeasurably easier will be one incontrovertible fact: eleven other people, many of whom must be as intelligent as he, heard the same testimony and saw the same evidence and came to a common conclusion. Isn't it likely, therefore, that their verdict and not his is the correct one?

Most juries that are at first divided much more evenly than eleven to one eventually reach a stage in deliberations when they, too, face a single holdout. In such situations much of the above applies, but a juror who at one time had allies seems to gain tenacity from that support even after it has vanished. He is much more likely to remain a minority of one forever—that is, until the court accepts a hung jury. In union there is strength, and somehow when *two* jurors share the unpopular position, their power is more than twice as great as that of the lonely holdout. Thus, a ten to two vote at the outset is much closer to a nine to three or an eight to four vote in its effect upon the course and duration of the jury's debate.

"Debate"—the very word suggests two sides that are more or less evenly matched, and for a jury's deliberations to be thought of as a debate we must assume that the weak side consists of at least two people. Given that, of one thing these minority jurors can be sure: at some point they will be put on the defensive. For a second fundamental rule of jury behavior is that the minority must eventually try to justify its position to the majority. A third rule is that the greater the number of people in the minority, the easier it will be for them to defend their position successfully. But a well-documented finding considerably dilutes the importance of both these rules; in most cases a jury's first ballot—assuming, of course, that it is not a tie—indicates what the final verdict will be. Even if, allowing for some "undecideds," one side takes the initial lead by merely a single vote, that side will probably prevail in the end.

To understand why this usually happens and why it occasionally does not, let us imagine some jury deliberations and comment on each one in turn. For our first case we'll go back to the robbery charge against the young man who was arrested after he had been seen throwing a gun (or was it a bottle?) in the bushes. We'll call him Lenny. The jury, having just taken its opening vote, finds itself divided six for conviction, three for acquittal, three undecided. The forewoman, who was elected to that position and belongs to the majority, begins the discussion:

The Case of the Gun in the Bushes

Forewoman: Since most of us have already made up our minds one way or the other, I think we should hear first from the people who are undecided. Let's see what's troubling them so that maybe we can resolve their doubts. Mr. Sloane?

Sloane: I dunno. I guess I gotta believe the cop who says he saw the kid throw the gun in the bushes. But it beats me how this guy who was just held up can make an identification that ain't worth a pile of beans. The kid was two feet away from him, pokin' a gun in his gut—no mask, no hat, nothin'. It wasn't even dark yet. Then he gets on the stand and says he can't be sure it was this Lenny.

Forewoman: But of course he refused to say it *wasn't* Lenny.

Kilpatrick: And he did say that the holdup man was about Lenny's size and was wearing exactly what Lenny had on when he was arrested.

Loos: A T-shirt and jeans. Big deal. What kid doesn't wear a T-shirt and jeans today?

Forewoman: The *important* thing is that the poor man was frozen with fear. He was so scared he didn't see clearly. It's no wonder that he doesn't trust his memory.

Baron: It doesn't seem to occur to you that maybe he couldn't identify Lenny because he'd never seen him before.

Rapp: C'mon now. We agreed we'd hear from the undecided folks before we started arguing.

Forewoman: Yes. Mrs. Gilman?

Gilman: To be perfectly frank, I must say I have this gut feeling that Lenny is guilty, but I just wish there were some more

—y'know—hard evidence against him, not just the testimony of one policeman. It doesn't seem enough to convict him on, y'know. Just one policeman. Couldn't they have—

Kilpatrick (interrupting): But not just any policeman. This officer has been decorated for bravery.

Loos: What the hell's that got to do with it? So five years ago he chased some hoodlum across the roof and gunned him down. That don't mean he couldn't make a mistake when he caught this kid.

Forewoman: I agree that his award isn't terribly relevant but I think his superb record is. And when it comes down to his word against Lenny's—well, really, I don't see that there's much choice.

Gilman: You're right, I guess. And Lenny had no alibi at all. Let me think about it some more.

Forewoman: Mr. Solow, you're one of the undecideds, aren't you?

Solow: Yup.

Forewoman: What's preventing you from making up your mind?

Solow: I like the kid.

Loos: So do I.

Forewoman (ignoring Loos): You *like* Lenny?

Solow: Yeah, he seems like a decent kid to me.

Kilpatrick: Then what was he doing with ninety-seven dollars in his pocket? Where would a kid like that get that kind of money?

Solow: Well, he said he won it in a football pool.

Rapp: And you buy that? C'mon now.

Gilman: Y'know, I forgot about that and it upset me terribly when I heard it. He shouldn't have been betting in the first place. But to try to make us believe he won almost a hundred dollars

. . . why, my son once won a baseball pool and I think it was all of twenty dollars.

Baron: There are, of course, many different kinds of betting pools and some—

Sloane (interrupting): I been in all kinds and never won a dime. Come off it. The kid's lyin'—just like he is when he says he was runnin' 'cuz he was late for supper. In a family like that it don't matter when people eat. They eat whenever they want. Ain't no such thing as bein' late.

Baron: How do you know so much about Lenny's family?

Loos: Yeah, you one of the neighbors?

Sloane: God forbid. And never mind how I know, I know. And I'm voting guilty now.

Gilman: Yes, I think I am, too.

Lenny is probably doomed. The vote is now eight for conviction, three for acquittal, one undecided. The latter, Mr. Solow, will probably fall into line soon since his doubt rests solely on his personal reaction to the defendant. While such instinctive feelings should not be discounted, they tend to collapse when they are challenged by a hard and insistent emphasis on the evidence. And the evidence is surely not in Lenny's favor. Aside from his denial of guilt, his defense seems to consist of not much more than the victim's failure to make an absolute identification of him. The state, for its part, may not have mustered all that powerful an attack, but it has succeeded in persuading a majority of the jurors. Let's examine how the leaders of that majority went about increasing their numbers.

First, the leader, the forewoman, uses her position to assume immediate control. She is obviously vigorous, intelligent, and well-spoken—and wise enough to realize that she should concentrate on the line of least resistance. Instead of suggesting that the "undecideds" speak first, she could have had them listen to a discussion between the two opposing sides and make up their minds in that way. But no, she knows that it is best to get the momentum going by strengthening the majority as soon as possible. She knows further that the votes she needs are far more likely to come from the "undecideds" than from the "not-guilties."

Second, the forewoman and her chief "aide," Kilpatrick, make the most of what they've got. A tentative identification is better than none at all and one policeman of proven virtue and commendability can go a long way as a means of persuasion.

Third, the leaders of the majority use the jurors' common knowledge of life—that is, what they have learned by living and what they have experienced—to bolster their arguments. Nothing was said in the courtroom about the victim's being so "frozen with fear" that his perception was impaired. (For a prosecution witness to be led to make such an admission would open all sorts of avenues to the defense.) But now that this possibility has been stated by a juror as an emphatic truth, it seems beyond question: Of course a person could be so frightened he couldn't see straight. Similarly, while not all of us participate in betting pools, everyone knows the odds are decidedly against those who do.

Fourth, by focusing on the "undecideds" and their doubts, the forewoman has in effect relegated the minority to the sidelines. Further weakened by their own personalities—the minority obviously does not have a leader who can break in and effectively take charge—they are reduced to muttering and heckling, voicing their objections to what is being said in a manner that seems almost calculated to offend their only conceivable source of reinforcement, the "undecideds."

And so the minority has lost two potential allies and will

probably soon lose the third. One of the not-guilties has not spoken at all, and if silence means growing uncertainty, she, too, may join the majority before long. That will leave only Mr. Loos and Mr. Baron, the possibility of a hung jury, or the greater likelihood of a unanimous conviction.

The Case of the Angry Drummer

Now let us return to the Case of the Angry Drummer. You'll recall that the defendant, whom we'll call Danny, has been charged with stabbing another member of his combo, the guitarist. Other relevant details will become apparent as we proceed. The jurors have begun their deliberations. They are split in equal thirds—four each for conviction and acquittal and four undecided. The foreman, the first juror chosen, is in the last faction:

Foreman: Hell, I'm so confused by this case I don't know where I am. And I never did like jazz.

Ellington: Well, one thing I think we can all agree on—before the defense called its first witness, this guy looked pretty guilty.

Goodman: I don't agree on that at all. I kept an open mind until I heard *all* the witnesses.

Kenton: Well, *I* agree. I may be undecided now but until the day before yesterday I thought this was an open-and-shut case. Let's just consider what the D.A. proved.

Brown: Not much except that the guitar player was stabbed.

Foreman: There must have been more than that. The D.A. never shut up. Did you ever hear a guy talk so much? Anyway, I think Mrs. Kenton has the right idea. Take it, Sally.

Kenton: Well, first we heard about the argument that Danny got into with the guitar player. Three witnesses said they heard Danny threaten him. What was it he said?

Ellington: "Just watch out, you creep. I'm going to get you yet."

Brown: Oh, that doesn't mean a thing. You can't convict a man for that. We all go through life making empty threats when we're really angry.

James: Yeah, but the people we threaten don't usually wind up with knives sticking out below their shoulder blades.

Kenton: May I continue, please. The same three witnesses all said that after the fight Danny ran out of the club. I think one of them said "with fire in his eyes."

Foreman: Uh huh. That was the poetic shoe manufacturer.

Goodman: All of which only goes to prove that Danny was angry at the guitar player. And that's all the D.A. proved.

James: How the hell can you say that?

Brown: It's true, that's how.

Kenton: You can't completely disregard the testimony of the victim.

Shaw: I don't trust him at all.

Dorsey: What's to trust? You think he was lying about that shiv in his back?

Kenton: The fact is that he couldn't make a positive identification—which I think is strange.

Shaw: Exactly.

Ellington: It was dark. Danny jumped him from behind. After waiting for him in the alley there. Why is that so strange?

Brown: Because they struggled for a while before the guitar player was stabbed. I just don't believe you can wrestle with somebody you've known for fifteen years and not recognize him. I don't care how dark it was in the alley . . . and there was some light.

Dorsey: One lousy bulb.

Thornhill: Look, I'm undecided. I don't know much about jazz musicians and the kind of life they lead but I suspect it's, well, you know, unsavory—drugs, all kinds of drugs, booze—you know. . . .

Dorsey: Okay, we know. Get to the point.

Thornhill: Well, I happen to think Mr. Brown is right. That fellow must have recognized Danny if it was Danny. But if it was, why doesn't he say so? And if it wasn't, why doesn't he say *that?*

Shaw: Because there's a lot more to this case than we're being told. Probably the D.A. doesn't even know half of it.

Brown: I'll bet you're right. It's a tip of the iceberg situation. We see this bit at the top—

Kenton: And even that's not clear.

Brown: But the bulk of it is under the water.

Dorsey: Forget the iceberg. What about the button?

Brown: Totally worthless as proof of anything.

James: How the hell can you say that?

Brown: Because if there are *two* guys in the band with jackets that are missing buttons, by sheer logic there has to be a reasonable doubt about whether the button belonged to either one of them. There's no more than a fifty–fifty chance that the button was from Danny's jacket. I certainly hope we're not going to convict when we're faced with those odds.

Ellington: You're forgetting that the other guy, the bass player, didn't have a motive and Danny most assuredly did.

Thornhill: But how do you know that the bass player had no motive? He was never even called to the stand. The defense produces this housekeeper from the hotel who testifies that the bass player asked her to sew a button on his jacket the day after the stabbing. Period. That's all we heard about the bass player.

Foreman: Maybe he plays too low. Mrs. Kenton, do you want to continue—

Kenton: Yes, but I should say that I *was* disturbed by the D.A.

not calling the bass player as a witness. How *did* he lose that button?

Dorsey: It fell off—what's the big deal?

Thornhill: Then why wasn't he asked to say that on the stand?

Dorsey: What's the matter? The trial didn't go on long enough?

James: This jury duty's cost me plenty. A helluva lot of difference one more witness would have made.

Thornhill: He could have made a lot of difference to me.

James: I think to me, too. Even when I was voting for guilty something in the back of my mind was bugging me. I know now. It's that damned bass player. Why the hell didn't he testify?

Brown: And that's just one of the mysteries. This case is loaded with them. How can we convict?

Kenton: I think we should take another vote.

Thornhill: I agree.

Foreman: Okeydokey.

It looks as if Danny the Drummer is going to beat the rap. On the next vote, three of the original "undecideds" (the foreman, Kenton, and Thornhill) and one of the original "guilties" (James) join the four "not-guilties" (Goodman, Brown, Shaw, and one who shall be forever nameless), making the tally eight not guilty, three guilty, one undecided. Let's see how the tide was made to turn so impressively.

First, the foreman, who with his feeble jokes would probably be happier as the M.C. at a summer resort, has in effect abdicated his leadership responsibility. This is due partly to his nonchalant and offhand manner, partly to the fact that he is confused by the case. But he has the wit to turn the reins over to someone capable of bringing structure to the discussion, Mrs. Kenton. When a jury is so sharply divided, a disorganized debate can ramble on for hours without bringing the group an inch closer to a unanimous verdict.

Second, this segment of deliberation shows how key roles may be played by those who would be least expected to play them, the "undecideds." From the foreman, who recognizes his limitations, to Kenton, who has a methodical mind and a firm, nononsense way about her, to Thornhill, who, while admitting his puzzlement, asks the right questions, we have a trio whose very undecidedness points up the weakness of the state's case. By definition, "undecided" means doubtful. Once doubt was expressed by more than one person, it was intensified simply from the fact that it was shared. Since there was no one on the "guilty" side who could explain away the doubt, it gained the power to move four people to the opposing side.

Third, the authentic leader of the "not-guilties," Brown, uses every opportunity to remind the other jurors of what is at stake. Rather than allow his colleagues—those with him as well as those against him—to get so embroiled in details that they forget the purpose of their deliberations, Brown is constantly referring to the possibility of conviction. Seen in that perspective, reasons for doubt grow immeasurably in importance.

Fourth, when a jury is eager to hear from a witness who, for reasons unknown to them, is never called to testify, the absence is often more conspicuous, and more memorable, than the presence of many of the witnesses who take the stand. Furthermore, the nonappearance tends to damage materially the case for the side that should have called the witness—in this instance, the prosecution. If Danny the Drummer is acquitted, he will probably owe his freedom to the bass player who lost a button and missed the trial.

The Case of Nathaniel Trueblood

For our next venture inside a jury room, we'll invent a situation unlike any that we have considered before. Welcome to the world of white-collar crime. Here no acts of violence are committed and no one looks upon a defendant with fear, disgust, or loathing. The alleged offenses involve the illegal gain of money or other property, but not the use of weapons or brute force; the persons accused are usually well dressed, well spoken, and well respected. When such people are on trial, jurors face a challenge that, in subtle but significant ways, is quite different from the task of rendering judgment on those who are poor, uneducated, disreputable, or—for whatever reason—inescapably suspect. Indeed, a defendant whom they would not have hesitated to invite into their homes tests the prejudices of his jurors just as severely as does a teenager from the ghetto.

Who wouldn't be delighted to have as a dinner guest our next defendant, a former Congressman of the United States? We'll call him Nathaniel Trueblood; until a year ago, when he chose not to run for reelection, he was an honored member of the House of Representatives from a sparsely populated western state. Now accused of having accepted a sizable campaign contribution from a foreign source during his last congressional race, which is a violation of federal law, Trueblood is being tried in a city that he once represented in Washington. Although it is not his hometown, everyone on the jury knew him at least by reputation long before he was even indicted. The trial has been covered by press from all over the country, leaving limited seating in the courtroom for the hundreds of would-be spectators. The jurors have just retired; they are led by an elected foreman who calls for an immediate vote. The tally stands at seven for acquittal, five for conviction. The foreman is one of the seven.

Foreman: Seven to five. I'd say we have our work cut out for us. Could one of you who voted guilty tell me what you think Nat Trueblood is guilty of?

Fillmore: Is that a serious question?

Foreman: You're damned right it's serious. What *in your opinion* did Nat Trueblood do to warrant conviction?

Fillmore: Exactly what the United States government says he did—he accepted $25,000 for his last election campaign from a guy from the Philippines. And that, my friend, is against the law.

Foreman: And you want to convict him for that?

Wilson: If we believe Trueblood took the money, how can we *not* convict him?

Foreman: Easy. He probably did take the Filipino's money, but I voted for not guilty and I'll keep on voting that way 'til hell freezes over.

Fillmore: You can't be serious.

Foreman: I sure am.

Grant: Well then, we'd better tell the judge right now that we're a hung jury because I for one will hold out as long as you will.

Tyler: No point in doing anything as rash as that. The judge won't accept it. He'll make us sit here for hours anyway.

Hayes: Maybe days. Mr. Grant, what the foreman here is trying to say is that while technically speaking, Trueblood may have broken the law, there are—well, let's say, extenuating circumstances that affect his vote—and mine, too.

Tyler: Right.

McKinley: Correct.

Grant: This is very interesting. Can I ask for a show of hands from all those who voted not guilty—

Foreman (interrupting): About what?

Grant: I'd like to know how many of the seven of you believe

Trueblood accepted that illegal campaign contribution.

Foreman (raising his hand high): No doubt about it in my mind. (Five other jurors raise their hands.)

Grant: Mr. Harrison, I think you're the only one who voted to acquit who didn't raise his hand.

Harrison: That's real observant of you, Mr. Grant. Fact is I'm not sure whether Nat took the 25 Gs or not. The Feds never did care for a maverick like him and I didn't like the way they used that Mr. Wisealeck. I'd trust him about as far as I can throw a horse.

Grant: By Mr. Wisealeck I assume you mean Mr. Weisweiler.

Harrison: I mean the critter who got immunity for sitting up there and saying just what the government wanted him to say.

Tyler: What a weasel he was.

McKinley: Weasel? I've known skunks that smelled better than Weisweiler.

Hayes: I'll bet his own mother couldn't stay in the same room with him.

Grant: It seems to me we're missing the point. We don't have to like Weisweiler to believe him, and the fact that he was granted immunity certainly doesn't mean he was lying.

Harrison: Well, that's right, Mr. Grant, but it sure gives him a reason for lying, doesn't it? The government's promise not to prosecute him for his part in this thing.

Fillmore: Not a word of his testimony could be shaken—don't forget that.

Grant: Seems to me when you're reciting a made-up story, it's easier to be steady about it than when you're trying to recollect what really happened.

Fillmore: What about all the other witnesses who confirmed Weisweiler's testimony? I didn't hear anything in that courtroom that made me think Weisweiler was lying or Trueblood was innocent.

Harrison: Never said he's innocent. Just not convinced he's guilty, that's all. And even if he did take that money, with Mr. Wisealeck encouraging him, he needed it. He was in a helluva tough election fight that year, needed every damn penny he could lay his hands on if he was gonna win.

Grant: And you think that excuses his crime?

Foreman: Mr. Grant, the way I see it a man's life is a balance sheet. On one side you can tote up all the good things he's done, and on the other all the bad. Now do you agree that Nat Trueblood's life is just about over?

Grant: I'm not sure about that. He still may—

Fillmore: He looked like death sitting there.

Foreman: The man's like the broken limb of a birch tree—all skinny and bent and pale gray.

Hayes: I can remember him when he was in his prime. What a speaker! He was a wizard with words.

Wilson: He certainly didn't have much to say on the witness stand.

Fillmore: You had to strain to hear him.

Wilson: All those "I don't recall's," and "My memory is vague about that."

Grant: Let's face it—he had no case.

Foreman: He has something more important than a case: the debt we all owe him. On that balance sheet I was talking about, there's plenty on the bad side, including accepting this illegal contribution, but there's a lot more on the good side. Let me ask all of you who're voting guilty—do you have any idea what Nat Trueblood has done for this state in the thirty years he was in Congress, especially for the folks in this here county?

Grant: Please remember the judge's instructions—that has absolutely nothing to do with these deliberations. We're not concerned with how many dams he had built or how much government money he brought in. All that stuff his lawyer was throwing at us in his summation—that's just a bunch of baloney. How come the lawyer didn't even mention what went on at those meetings with the Filipino? That's what's important. Trueblood isn't being tried for his record in Congress.

Hayes: Who says?

Grant: The court. You heard the judge. He's on trial for—

McKinley: Spare us, please. We all know about the fifty-two counts in the indictment. And it seems to me we're all missing the point. The foreman touched on it but didn't pursue it. Trueblood is a dying man. He didn't run for Congress last time—

Grant (interrupting): Because he knew the government was building this case against him.

McKinley: Maybe so, but I don't think he would have run if his past was as clean and sweet as mountain roses. He's seventy-four years old—

Harrison (interrupting): And ailing.

McKinley: Correct. So I have two questions for you people who are voting for conviction. Do you want to send a sick old man to prison—even for one day? And if you do, what do you hope to accomplish by that? Mr. Grant?

Grant: I'm in favor of convicting the man, and I'll leave the rest of it to the judge. Let him give Trueblood a suspended sentence if he chooses.

Fillmore: That's fine with me.

Foreman: I don't think we can take that chance.

Harrison: Hell, no. That judge looks like a hanging judge to me.

Hayes: I'm guessing he'll think he has to make an example of Trueblood.

Foreman: That's my feeling, too. He's out to strike a blow against corruption in government—and he'll strike Nat Trueblood right into the slammer.

Johnson: You really think he'll do that?

McKinley: Of course, there's no way of knowing for certain. But my objection goes deeper than that. I refuse to allow this man who has done so much for us all—so much for his country, if I may say so—to go to his grave condemned by twelve of his fellow citizens. I believe that no important purpose will be served by blemishing his record in this disgraceful way.

Grant: But, damn it, the man has stained his own record. You all admit, except maybe for Mr. Harrison, that he accepted that money. None of *us* forced him to commit a crime.

Fillmore: He did it of his own free will.

Grant: Exactly. And the law demands that we discharge only one responsibility: reach a decision as to whether he's guilty of this crime or not. That's all we're supposed to do. The consequences of our decision—

McKinley (interrupting): A mark against the name of Trueblood throughout history.

Wilson: I think you're getting a little dramatic there.

Johnson: Finish what you were gonna say, Mr. Grant, about the consequences of our decision.

Grant: Just that the consequences of our decision should not concern us to the point where we become blind to the primary reason we're here.

Johnson: That's what I thought you were gonna say and I gotta disagree. Laws don't exist in a vacuum and neither do we. We *have* to think of the consequences of our verdict. We're gonna ruin the remaining years of that man if we find him guilty, whether the judge sends him to the pen or not, and I don't think I wanna have a hand in that.

Fillmore: You voted for guilty.

Johnson: Yeah, well, I'm not gonna do it again.

Former Representative Trueblood is not destined for the penitentiary. He will not be found guilty. Mr. Grant and Mr. Fillmore will hold out for that verdict as long as they have breath, and, thus, the jury will be deadlocked at ten for acquittal, two for conviction. Faced with a hung jury, the judge will declare a mistrial; the government, however, will not subject this "sick old man" to another trial. Whatever blemishes there may be on his record, a conviction on this charge will not be among them.

From Mr. Grant's strictly legalistic point of view, this jury was responsible for a miscarriage of justice. After hearing and seeing all the evidence against the defendant, every juror except one believed him guilty and that one, Mr. Harrison, had only the shakiest ground for doubt. Yet the initial majority not only refused to convict, they succeeded in increasing their number as the deliberations progressed. How did they manage this and why weren't they successful in bringing in a not-guilty verdict?

First, the jury here was dealing with a case that in one major respect was unique among the legal contests that are discussed in this chapter and, indeed, in this book: a modern trial that, because of the defendant's prominence, has captured the interest of the public and therefore the attention of the news media. This fact casts all sorts of shadows on the proceedings in the courtroom and in the jury room.

We did not concern ourselves with the problem of jury selection, but we can easily imagine how difficult it must have been to find more than twelve people (including alternates) who would even claim to be unbiased in judging a man who had served them in Congress for thirty years. Furthermore, the publicity generated by the trial imposed on the chosen jurors an unavoidable and constant awareness of the consequences of their verdict. Who really cared whether Danny the Drummer was convicted? Aside from Danny himself and perhaps some relatives and friends, nobody. To the jurors in this case, the whole world and—to at least one of them—history seemed to be waiting anxiously for their decision.

But most important of all the considerations that arise when a defendant is well known is the prejudgment that a juror is almost certain to have made before the trial begins. This prejudgment does not necessarily relate to the defendant's guilt or innocence (if it does and the prospective juror answers truthfully during the *voir dire,* he or she will not be sitting on the jury); it relates to how the defendant is viewed as a person. To the majority of the jurors Nat Trueblood was a hero, appreciated, admired, beloved. This was, quite plainly, a prejudice in the defendant's favor shared by seven jurors. In effect, their personal feelings about the man made his conviction—no matter what the evidence against him—an impossibility.

Second, by acknowledging Trueblood's guilt from the start, the majority changed the focus of the deliberations from a jury's customary concern—Did the defendant do it?—to the more unusual question—What will be the effect of his conviction? Confronted by this, the minority was forced to justify its position (as almost all jury minorities are) in a way it was unprepared to handle. Grant and Fillmore could certainly have demonstrated how powerful was the government's case; they could not, and did not, show how Trueblood's conviction would benefit anyone. Failing in that task, they were inevitably weakened by defections.

Third, jurors tend to distrust witnesses who testify for the state in exchange for a promise of immunity from prosecution. Since they would not face prosecution if they were not themselves likely law-breakers, the honesty of such witnesses is immediately suspect. Further, as Harrison noted, they may have good reason to lie. Finally, very often such witnesses were closely associated with the defendant in the crime that is charged; thus, there is an element of betrayal in their testimony. The abuse that the jurors heaped on Mr. Weisweiler stemmed from all of these factors, but only Harrison was so influenced by them that he refused to acknowledge the defendant's guilt. Often, when "immunized" witnesses are crucial to the state's case, that case is lost to the prosecution because jurors react with such distaste to testimony that they consider to have been "bought"—and delivered by someone beneath contempt.

Fourth, from Grant's "bunch of baloney" comment we know that the defense in its summation emphasized Trueblood's accomplishments as a legislator and made little effort to refute the prosecution. The attorney was thus building on the sympathy for his client that he, quite correctly, assumed to exist among many if not all of the jurors. Grant and others could argue that Trueblood's past services to the state were irrelevant to the case at hand. But the majority refused to hold to such a narrow view. Because the man on trial was known to them, they could not limit themselves to judging only the facts that had been presented in court. For them, Trueblood's entire career was at issue, not simply the question of whether or not he had accepted an illegal campaign contribution. While this may seem comparable to changing the rules in the middle of a game, the majority would argue that a man was on trial, not a legal abstraction, and that a man would have to suffer the consequences of the jury's decision. Therefore, everything that related to this man became relevant, including his age, his health, and his record in Congress. If, as in most trials, the defendant had been a total stranger to the jurors, such factors would not carry as much weight. But when jurors can look upon—or can be made to look upon—a defendant not simply as a person accused of breaking a law, but as a person they can identify with—when, indeed, they can picture themselves sitting in that chair at the defense table—then the only rules that count are those by which they would want to be judged themselves.

Fifth, although we ended our deliberations long before the jury admitted defeat, we can easily conjure up the scene in the jury room as the possibility of deadlock loomed. Grant and Fillmore were determined to discharge their responsibilities exactly as they understood them. Neither had any intention of going beyond the immediate facts of the case and voting for acquittal on the basis of "irrelevant" circumstances. Nor would they vote for acquittal in order to please the majority and "get it over with." So they held out to the end and eventually they left the courthouse feeling that they had preserved their own integrity and, perhaps, even the integrity of the jury system. Among any group there may be one or two such uncompromising people of principle. In history they are often the martyrs whom later generations revere. In a jury room, if they cannot prevail, they are often the "stubborn mules" who, from the point of view of the other jurors, waste the court's time and the taxpayers' money.

The Case of the Missing Motive

As another example of a jury at work, let us consider deliberations in which compromise becomes the order of the day. We'll return to the case of the young man—let's call him Paul—who, accused of having shot and wounded his aunt, faces a four-count indictment (attempted murder, assault in the first and second degree, possession of a gun). Because this fact is crucial to the jury's deliberations, we must mention that Paul is black, as is one of the jurors, Mrs. Jackson. All the other jurors are white. The foreman is the first-chosen juror, and we begin at the beginning.

Foreman: Does anyone want to suggest how we should proceed? (Silence.) In that case, let's just go around the table and find out what everybody thinks. We'll start on my right. Mrs. Lee?

Lee: I pass. I'm not sure what I think.

Foreman: Mr. Davis?

Davis: I think he shot her, but I'm not sure he wanted to kill her.

Foreman: You want to elaborate on that?

Davis: Just that I can't believe a woman wouldn't know her own nephew.

Foreman: Right. Mr. Stuart?

Stuart: I think the kid shot her and I think he wanted to kill her––because you don't shoot people only to inconvenience them a little bit.

Jackson: I agree with you on that last part, and that's why I don't think Paul had anything to do with the shooting.

Foreman: You're speaking out of turn, Mrs. Jackson. We'll get to you in a moment. Mr. Stephens?

Jackson (muttering): What is this, some sort of a classroom?

Foreman: In my judgment, we'll make better progress if on this first go-round everybody speaks in turn. Then when we have an idea of how seriously divided we are, we can get into a general discussion. Mr. Stephens?

Stephens: About all that I'm willing to vote guilty on is gun possession. None of the rest of it has been proved, at least not to my satisfaction.

Foreman: Interesting. Miss Hood.

Hood: From the moment I laid eyes on him I thought he was guilty. We'll be saving lives if we can put him behind bars.

Jackson: Why don't we just take him out and shoot him now? Save all that trouble and money keeping him in prison.

Foreman: Mrs. Jackson, please. Can we proceed? Mr. Booth?

Booth: I pass. Undecided.

Foreman: On all counts?

Booth: On all counts.

Foreman: Mr. Bragg?

Bragg: Well, I have to believe the boy was there. But otherwise I'm—

Jackson: Why? Why do you *have* to believe that Paul was there?

Foreman: Mrs. Jackson, please let us finish this first go-round.

Stuart: Yeah. Let's find out exactly where we stand.

Foreman: Mr. Benjamin?

Benjamin: Not guilty—on all counts.

Foreman: Well. Mr. Hunter?

Hunter: Not guilty of attempted murder. Guilty of everything else.

Booth: I don't understand how he can be guilty of both assault one and assault two.

Jackson: You're speaking out of turn, Mr. Booth. Teacher says we have to hear from Mrs. Memminger before you get a second chance.

Memminger: I pass.

Foreman: Undecided?

Memminger: I didn't say that. I just want to hear from Mrs. Jackson before I—

Jackson (interrupting): My turn at last. Not guilty, on all counts.

Foreman: Well, my own vote is for guilty across the board. And from the way I tally it there are two others who agree with me completely, three who agree with me partially, two who disagree entirely, and four who haven't committed themselves as yet. Now, Mrs. Jackson, what else do you want to say?

Jackson: I want to say that Paul didn't try to kill that woman, that he didn't shoot her, and that he wasn't even on her porch that night.

Davis: You're saying then that the woman wouldn't recognize her own nephew.

Jackson: Oh, she'd recognize him all right if he was there, but he wasn't.

Stuart: You're saying then that she's lying.

Jackson: You got it. That's what I'm saying.

Foreman: Tell us, please, why is she lying?

Jackson: I have no idea, sir. But since you think he shot her, you tell me why he did.

Foreman: Unfortunately no motive was ever offered in testimony, but—

Jackson (interrupting): You can say that again.

Lee: That's precisely what troubles me so. This is a crime without a motive.

Benjamin: And there's no such thing unless a defendant is crazy, and Paul isn't crazy. If the D.A. with that Phi Beta Kappa key hanging from his belly can't come up with a motive, I'm not convicting the kid of anything.

Jackson: Right on.

Stuart: I was afraid we'd get bogged down in this matter of motive. As I see it, we're intelligent, sophisticated people, and we know that in families there are all kinds of conflicts that people don't want to talk about openly, on the witness stand or anywhere else. Maybe Paul thought his aunt was trying to take his father away from his mother. Who knows—?

Hood (interrupting): Exactly. Those last two words are the key. Who knows? With all due regard for you, Mrs. Jackson, I don't think white people can even begin to know the way black people think and what prompts them to do certain things. We can speculate all day and all night on why this scum shot his aunt, but we've been told it's not our job to come up with a motive and it's not. We have to deal with the facts we've been given and with Paul himself.

Davis: I can go along with you about the facts, but if you don't have a motive, how can you be sure that he wanted to kill her? Okay, he shot the gun, but maybe he was scared into doing it.

Stuart: Like I said before, people who shoot guns shoot to kill.

Davis: Well, I'm not prepared to apply that generalization to this case.

Foreman: What are you prepared to do?

Davis: What I said before—vote not guilty of attempted murder, guilty of everything else.

Booth: Do you know what you're saying—that he's guilty on both assault counts? That's impossible. That flies in the face of all logic. He either intended to inflict serious bodily injury or he didn't. If he did, you have to find him guilty of assault one and not guilty of assault two.

Hood: I don't want to find him not guilty of anything.

Benjamin: And I don't want to find him guilty of anything.

Stephens: So you agree with Mrs. Jackson that the aunt is lying, that Paul wasn't even there that night.

Jackson: Don't forget that the neighbor lady testified that she saw someone running away from the house that night and it wasn't Paul, and she's known him all his life.

Stuart: So has the aunt. It's the victim's word against the neighbor's—and which one was closer? Which one could make the more reliable identification?

Jackson: And which one has more reason to lie?

Hood: We can't know the answer to that. Who's to say what kind of relationship there was between Paul and that neighbor?

Benjamin: She's old enough to be his grandmother.

Hood: She may be his grandmother. Who knows? We have to deal with what we do know: a woman was shot and she later identified the boy who shot her as her own nephew. There was absolutely no doubt in her mind, she said, and there isn't in mine, either.

Bragg: She was a convincing witness, all right.

Booth: I agree she was a convincing witness. I'll even say Paul shot her, but can someone explain to me how he can be guilty of both first and second degree assault?

Foreman: If we find him guilty of attempted murder, the other counts become meaningless. If I can tell the judge right now that we've reached a guilty verdict on the first count, I assure you the trial will be over and we'll be able to go home.

Jackson: I say to you now, I will never vote the boy guilty of attempted murder.

Benjamin: Neither will I.

The discussion continues. Mr. Booth, the logician, announces that he will vote guilty on gun possession and assault two, not guilty on the other counts. Mr. Bragg goes along; believing as he does that Paul was on the porch that night, he must assume that the boy, at the very least, shot the gun. But he will assume nothing else. Mrs. Lee, while still troubled by the absence of a motive, cannot doubt the aunt's identification of Paul as her assailant and, therefore, will also vote to convict on the two lesser counts. Mrs. Memminger finally speaks up and says the discussion has convinced her that the state has a very weak case and therefore she will vote not guilty on all counts.

It is time for a dinner recess. Guards accompany the jurors to a restaurant across the street from the courthouse. There they are admonished to say nothing about the case and to keep their meal bills below ten dollars.

Back in the jury room, the jurors are in a more relaxed frame of mind, and the foreman suggests they immediately take a formal vote on each count of the indictment. The tally is as follows:

Attempted murder—three guilty, nine not guilty.

Assault in the first degree—five guilty, seven not guilty.

Assault in the second degree—eight guilty, four not guilty.

Possession of a gun—nine guilty, three not guilty.

Foreman: I guess you could say we're split down the middle.

Stuart: I don't understand how anyone can vote guilty on gun possession and not guilty on everything else.

Hood: Really, Mr. Stephens, can you explain why he would have the gun if not to shoot it?

Stephens: I'm not being logical, I know—

Stuart: I'd say you're not being reasonable.

Stephens: You see, I have this feeling that the kid is guilty, but I don't think the D.A. has proved *anything* very conclusively. So, rather than let Paul off, I'm for convicting him on the most minor charge. That reasoning may not satisfy all of you, but it lets me live with my conscience. It's as simple as that.

Hood: Do you realize that if we convict on the gun count alone, the judge will undoubtedly send this animal right back into the streets? He'll be put on probation or get a suspended sentence.

Stephens: That's up to the judge. I'll have done my duty as I see fit.

Hood: You don't feel you have any responsibility to the community, do you?

Stephens: Look, I don't know why you're picking on me. There are at least three people here who won't convict "this animal," as you call him, of anything. Why don't you work on them?

Jackson: Because she knows she won't get anywhere with us. She's a racist.

Hood: I was expecting that. It's not true of course. I have nothing against blacks. But that boy reeks of guilt. Not because of his color, but because of his expression and his manner. And those darting eyes as he spoke his lies up there on the witness stand—those black, piercing, darting eyes. It was as if he'd like to murder every one of us. I'll bet there's not a person in this room who wouldn't run the other way if they saw him coming toward them on a dark street, with that arrogant swagger of his. God, I hate him!

Benjamin (after a long silence): He still must be presumed innocent until *proven* guilty.

Hood: I have all the proof I need and so do most of us. If the rest of you are blind to what was apparent in the courtroom, you must be equally blind to what's going on in the world outside.

Memminger: This kind of discussion is getting us nowhere. It disgusts me and after hearing it, if anything my position has hardened. I think we should tell the judge we're deadlocked.

Foreman: Not so fast. Let's try to look at this rationally. We've been handed four counts. Granted there's no chance in the world we'll agree on all of them, but maybe we can agree on some of them. I'm willing to change my vote on the attempted murder count if some of you others will convict on the lesser counts.

Hood: Why, that's the most unprincipled thing I've ever heard in my life! You believe he wanted to kill the woman, but you'll disregard that in order to reach a verdict. That's outrageous! You may be foreman, but I for one do not intend to follow—(There is a knock at the door. The foreman rises as the guard who is stationed outside unlocks the jury room door to admit the judge's clerk.)

Clerk (smiling): Well, how're you doing?

Foreman (resuming his seat): Not so hot.

Hood: Let's be honest. We're very close to complete deadlock.

Clerk: After a mere four hours? Why, that's no time at all.

Jackson: It seems like four days.

Clerk: Well, you started late and you may be tired. We'll give you another hour or so. Then, if you still haven't reached a decision, we'll put you up for the night and you can resume in the morning. How far apart are you, anyway?

Foreman: On which count? The closest we are is nine to three.

Clerk: Hmmm. Well, this motel you'll be going to isn't bad. It's got beds with these magic fingers, y'know? Very relaxing. I guess you'll need that. Well, keep plugging away—for another hour at least. (He exits.)

Hood: I hope if we're sequestered we each have private rooms.

Lee: I think the very idea of being sequestered is terribly unfair. If we can't agree, we can't agree. Let us go home. I haven't been separated from my husband for a single night since we've been married.

Stuart: Maybe it'll do you both good. (Mrs. Lee glares at him.) No offense intended.

Foreman: The point is that I don't think it will do *any of us* any good. In the morning we won't be any closer to agreement than we are now.

Booth: How can you be so sure?

Foreman: Because nobody here is going to change anybody

else's mind. We don't disagree on the testimony we heard. We all remember pretty much the same things being said by the witnesses, by the attorneys, by the judge. We just interpret what we heard differently.

Hood: And what we saw.

Foreman: That, too. So there's no point in my trying to convince Mr. Benjamin here that Paul is guilty. You either accept the aunt's testimony as the truth or you don't. I do. He doesn't.

Benjamin: That's right.

Stephens: There is, of course, the fact that the kid has no alibi to speak of. He says he was home alone at the time of the shooting. Period.

Jackson: Why is that so unbelievable?

Stephens: It's not so unbelievable, but it would sure have helped if someone had come forward to verify it.

Bragg: It would have helped if he'd had a decent lawyer, too. That's one thing we haven't even talked about. There's that hotshot D.A. insinuating that Paul has a string of juvenile arrests as long as your arm—

Memminger (interrupting): We were supposed to disregard that.

Bragg: You're right. You're absolutely right. At least the lawyer had enough sense to object when it was starting to get interesting.

Jackson: You know that was a court-appointed lawyer. He probably just finished law school.

Bragg: Well, he should go back for some more courses.

Hood: The attorneys are not on trial.

Bragg: My point is that if the kid had had a top-notch lawyer, we probably would have voted to acquit two hours ago.

Benjamin: It was the D.A. who offended me. I thought he was trying to railroad the boy right into the cooler. Whatever sympathy I have for Paul comes directly from that prosecution table.

Foreman (after a long pause): Mr. Benjamin, would you like to step into the bathroom with me?

Benjamin: Wow. That has to be the best offer I've had all evening, but I'm not that desperate. What's on your mind?

Foreman: I'd just like to talk to you privately for a moment.

Benjamin (smiling and getting to his feet): Okay. I'm bigger than you are, anyway. (He and the foreman cross the room to the lavatory.)

Davis: Don't stay in there too long. One of us may have to use it for more important functions.

While the foreman and Mr. Benjamin confer in the lavatory, the other jurors continue to talk about the attorneys, almost deliberately avoiding discussion of the case itself. A few, notably Mrs. Lee and Mr. Booth, show signs of growing impatience. She sighs a lot; he starts to pace around the room. After about ten minutes, the two men emerge from the lavatory.

Hood: Before we hear about the deal you tried to cook up in there, I repeat once again that I will never vote to acquit on the attempted murder charge. You should know that now. I'm sorry if it makes that lengthy visit to the men's room useless.

Jackson: It's a ladies' room, too.

Foreman: Just listen to what I have to say. Then all of you can give your views and we'll take another vote. Maybe then it'll be magic finger time or just maybe Mrs. Lee will be able to go home to her husband.

Lee: I can't be the only one who objects to being sequestered.

Foreman: Believe me, you're not. As I said before, I don't think anyone here can be persuaded to think differently on the basis of another prolonged discussion of the evidence. In a sense, then, we have nothing more to deliberate about. So I have proposed to Mr. Benjamin that instead of deliberating we negotiate, that we try to reach a compromise verdict that we can all subscribe to. I grant you it won't be easy. And that's why I chose to confer with someone who has voted to acquit right down the line. I figured that if he would give in on something, I would, too. And then maybe the rest of you who feel as he does would go along with him and those who feel as I do would go along with me. Mr. Benjamin, why don't you explain our compromise.

Benjamin: Well, I should start by saying that though I've been for acquittal, I never really felt totally certain the aunt was lying. If she was, why couldn't Paul's lawyer present us with a reason for her lying? He couldn't—or didn't, which is the same thing. And I was probably overly influenced by the brutal tactics of the D.A. So when I try to remove the indignation I've felt about the way the prosecution presented its case, I'm left with a strong suspicion that Paul was there that night and that he shot his aunt. Now if I could, I'd vote for conviction only on the gun possession charge, but, as somebody said before, that makes no sense —not to me anyway. If Paul was there with a gun and the woman was shot in the side, no one else could have pulled the trigger. I've therefore agreed with the foreman to vote not guilty on the first two counts and guilty on the lesser counts—and he has agreed to do the same.

Hood (to the foreman): You didn't.

Foreman: I'm afraid I did. I want to reach a verdict, tonight. Not one of us—not even you, Miss Hood—can be absolutely certain that Paul is guilty of attempted murder. I confess that I have less than a reasonable doubt that he's guilty, but in the interest of reaching agreement, I'll deliberately enlarge that doubt—just so that we can bring in a conviction of some kind.

Stuart: What you're saying makes perfect sense.

Lee: That's the way I've been voting all along.

Foreman: I know that and so have quite a few others. That's why I'm hoping this compromise will find general acceptance.

Jackson: If he only had an alibi. (To Mr. Benjamin) What kind of sentence you think he'll get on those two little counts?

Benjamin: Very light if it's a first offense. And, who knows?—maybe he deserves more.

Foreman (after a pause): If no one else has anything to say now, I'd like to take another vote, count by count, starting from the bottom and with a show of hands—if that's okay with everybody. (No one objects.) All right. On the charge of gun possession, all those in favor of guilty. (All hands are raised, Mrs. Jackson's the last.) On the charge of assault in the second degree, all those in favor of guilty. (Again all hands are raised, this time almost simultaneously.) On the charge of assault in the first degree, all those in favor of guilty. (Only Miss Hood raises her hand, thereby creating an uproar compounded of curses, cries of "Racist!" "Be reasonable!" "Don't you want to get out of here tonight?" "What the hell's the matter with you?" etc.)

Hood: I'm not surprised at your reaction. Since you are all so totally devoid of personal conviction, you can't possibly understand someone who holds firm to hers. But to please you all, I'll reconsider. (She smiles.) I'll change my vote to not guilty on the assault one charge. (There is a smattering of applause and a few shouts of "Hurray!")

Foreman: Okay, so we're unanimously acquitting on that count. Last one. On the charge of attempted murder, all those in favor of guilty. (Again only Miss Hood raises her hand but this time she is greeted with silence, punctuated by a few weary groans.)

Hood: And here I will stand my ground. I don't care if we are sequestered for five weeks, I will never back down.

Booth: But, damnit, do you realize how illogical you're being? You just voted not guilty on assault with intent to inflict serious bodily injury and guilty of attempted murder! You're an intelligent woman, how can you take a position like that?

Foreman: Without meaning to pressure you—

Hood: Hah!

Foreman: I must say that your votes are staggeringly inconsistent. If he meant to murder the poor woman, obviously he intended to inflict serious bodily injury.

Hood: I couldn't agree with you more. But I think it was Mr. Stephens who said before, in effect, that logic be damned—he had to worry about his conscience. Well, his conscience apparently didn't mind his adding another little guilty vote in there, but mine resists a second not guilty. The first one was just to appease you, knowing as I did that I would hold out for conviction on attempted murder. And I'm sure that none of you doubt now that I *will* hold out.

Foreman: There's nothing we can say to convince you.

Hood: Nothing. That boy is a menace, and I couldn't rest knowing that thanks to me he'll be walking the streets in a few months or maybe even a few weeks.

Jackson: Maybe even in a few hours.

Hood: God help us all.

Foreman: Well, I think if we have to, maybe we can sell this.

Booth: What do you mean?

Foreman: I mean that the judge may accept a deadlock on the first charge and our verdicts on the other three. It's as simple as that.

Jackson: Then what happens?

Foreman: If the D.A. wants to try Paul again on the attempted murder charge, he can. But then it'll be a problem for twelve other unfortunates, not for us. And they'll have to deal with only one count.

Stuart: Good luck to them.

Booth: But we'll be a laughingstock in that courtroom when we deliver a verdict like this—not guilty on assault one and deadlocked on attempted murder.

Foreman: Whoever cares will know that it was a compromise verdict—with somebody balking at the compromise.

Booth: I think it's shameful.

Foreman: Miss Hood, will you change your vote?

Hood: Certainly not.

Foreman: Well, then, there you have it. (He rises to call the guard.) We had to deal with what they gave us. Now they'll have to deal with what we give them. Let's go.

When the jury's verdict is announced, Paul's defense attorney immediately moves that the first count of the indictment be dismissed. The judge so rules. Although the district attorney vehemently objects and reserves the right to file a countermotion, Paul will never again be tried for attempted murder. A short time later he will, however, be sentenced to eighteen months in prison for his convictions on the two lesser counts. From that term the court will subtract the eleven months he has already spent in jail awaiting trial and sentencing, and thus he will, as Miss Hood feared, be back on the street within seven months.

But Mr. Booth's fears that the jury would be looked upon with ridicule prove unfounded. Experienced lawyers and jurists would not be shocked, bewildered, or even amused by the inconsistency inherent in the jury's first-count deadlock and second-count acquittal. Indeed, simply upon hearing that decision, a

sophisticated attorney could probably do a creditable job of sum-
marizing the script that you have just read. For when evidence
is confusing and contradictory and when neither defense nor
prosecution presents an overpowering case, juries often resort to
negotiated or compromise verdicts. Like many another decision
made by a committee, such verdicts may be awkward, ungainly,
and fully satisfying to no one. But they are an inevitable result
of the jury system, and, if nothing else, they put an end to the
pain of deliberation.

Because of the nature of the indictment and the crosscurrents
it created, we spent much more time in the jury room on Paul's
case than on the cases we considered earlier. And as these twelve
embattled people struggled to reach agreement, their methods
of argument, reasoning, persuasion, and resistance uncovered
many new and important facets of jury behavior, only a few of
which we can discuss here.

To take the most obvious one first, racial prejudice was alive
and flourishing in this jury room. Its chief exponent was, of
course, Miss Hood, but it would be naive to assume that no other
juror was infected by it. The venom that spilled out of the speech
ending with "God, I hate him!" caused no more, and no less, of
a reaction than stunned and total silence. But we can be sure that
Miss Hood's words evoked sympathetic echoes in the minds of
jurors who chose not to divulge all their secrets. But to say that
prejudice—be it against blacks, as it was here, or against any
other minority group—influences the thinking of jurors is not to
say that it determines the verdicts of juries. On occasion it certainly may; in years past it certainly did, perhaps frequently. But
as methods of selecting members of the jury pool have grown
increasingly democratic and, more important, as white society
has grown increasingly sensitive to racial discrimination, bigotry
in the jury room has tended to be masked and guarded and

decidedly subordinate to rational consideration of the evidence. It is this writer's belief (to be elaborated upon in the next chapter) that jury service brings out the best, not the worst, in most people. Surely that was true of Miss Hood's colleagues. Whatever one may think of the compromise they arrived at, it found its basis in the testimony that was presented in court rather than in the color of the defendant's skin.

Second, if the foreman of this jury was not a schoolteacher, as Mrs. Jackson suggested, he should have been. He controlled the jurors in much the same way that an effective teacher controls his or her students. When he made a decision regarding procedures, he asked the jurors for their approval, well aware that none would object. When he saw conflict arising, he held it at bay until, knowing at last exactly how serious it was, he was prepared to cope with it. Although in a highly polarized group he stood staunchly with one faction, he never allowed himself to be identified solely as the leader of that faction. Instead he remained, above all else, the leader of the entire jury, trying first to reach unanimity on his own terms, realizing quickly that that was impossible, moving then toward working out a compromise, and, finally, achieving that compromise. His was an award-winning performance.

Third, groups that are straining to resolve conflicts give low priority to concerns of logic and consistency. While some jurors may be fast to pounce upon contradictions in testimony, they will not mind cutting some corners in their own thinking in order to stand close to or with the majority, and they will mind even less if their colleagues do the same. Thus, Mr. Stephens was willing to acknowledge that Paul stood on his aunt's porch with gun in hand but resisted accepting the charge that the defendant shot the gun—even though both points derived from the same testimony. Similarly, only Mr. Booth seemed troubled by the fact that the two assault charges were mutually exclusive. Logically, and quite correctly, he recognized that a guilty vote on one required a not-guilty vote on the other. But was anyone listening? Did anyone care? And, of course, there was the final blow to Mr. Booth's sense of propriety: a decision that proclaimed the defendant innocent of intent to inflict serious bodily injury but implied he was perhaps guilty of intent to kill. If Mr. Booth had been a fighter as well as a logician, he would probably have deadlocked the jury on the assault one charge and thereby saved himself from appearing ridiculous in his own eyes, even if in no one else's.

Fourth, jurors are inclined to evaluate attorneys, which is at least *poetic* justice since, as we have seen, attorneys always evaluate jurors. A well-known defense attorney once defined a jury as "twelve people in search of the best lawyer." Is the comment accurate? Yes and no; it is dependent upon a multiplicity of factors in any given courtroom or jury room. As Miss Hood, in one of her more enlightened observations, remarked, "The attorneys are not on trial." But almost all the other jurors were apparently struck by the incompetence of Paul's counsel and at least one, Mr. Benjamin, admitted to have been negatively influenced by the overly aggressive approach of the prosecutor.

Jurors, by common and historic agreement, cannot be lawyers, but for many of them, service at their first trial becomes a crash course in criminal law or, at the very least, an introduction to courtroom techniques. If a juror is observant and quick-witted, he or she is sure to notice how the opposing attorneys conduct themselves and argue their cases; indeed, the lawyers' methods may be considerably more interesting than the substance of the trial itself. Theoretically, the more sensitive a juror is to legal ploys and tactics, the less influenced he or she will be by them. Mr. Benjamin, for example, recognized finally that he had allowed himself to be offended by the district attorney's manner of attack. In actual practice, however, the respective skills of the opposing attorneys may have a powerful effect on the way jurors view the evidence, the witnesses, and the defendant. As Mr. Bragg commented as he waited for the vote for conviction: "... if the kid had had a top-notch lawyer, we probably would have voted to acquit two hours ago."

Fifth, whether or not a juror has a happy home life, sequestration is almost always viewed as a fate to be avoided. In this case, the prospect of being put up for the night clearly drove the jurors to reach agreement much sooner than they would have otherwise. Here again is a circumstance that may have serious impact on a jury's verdict but not the slightest link to considerations of justice.

Why does sequestration have about as much appeal as an acute case of acne? In its most extreme form, which occurs, as we have noted, only when a trial is sensational enough to warrant extensive press coverage, sequestration completely isolates jurors from the world, or, to put it differently, it confines them to a tight little island that has very limited ties to the mainland. When the court decides that a trial requires a sequestered jury, prospective jurors are usually asked if they can accept this hardship and excused if they say they cannot. Those who are willing and then selected to make the sacrifice can look forward to an experience best described in the following account:

Jurors were driven to their homes on January 15, the first evening after they had been selected to serve, so that they could get a week's worth of clothing. They were returned to their homes for clean clothing on January 20 and January 27. ... Each juror was accompanied by a marshal on each trip ... and even the windows of the vans [were] covered with paper so a juror [could not] see a newspaper headline at a newsstand. The jurors also were escorted by marshals to two theater productions and to one dinner at a restaurant away from their hotel. . . . The jurors were allowed no visits by relatives and were allowed telephone conversations only after a deputy marshal dialed the number, cautioned the answering party against discussing the case, and listened in on a second telephone that had a cut-off button to be used if either party violated the restrictions.

What prompted such security measures was the month-long, front-page trial of a prominent political figure (which, incidentally, ended in a hung jury). But precautions like these will be familiar to anyone who has ever been on a sequestered jury. They are the components of a grand design to prevent jury tampering and to quarantine jurors against any outside influence that could, however remotely, affect their thinking and their judgment about the case on which they serve.

Because Paul's trial was not covered by the press, there was no recognizable need to sequester the jury—that is, not until after deliberations had begun—and, once selected, the jurors had probably never even entertained that possibility. Later, of course, it became quite real, looming as an unexpected and distressing threat. Suddenly, a new force was at work in the jury room, compelling the jurors to try to resolve their conflicts before they were all hauled away for the night.

There is one final observation to be made about Paul's jury. It is generally thought that in order to get a conviction, the prosecution must prove to the jury that the defendant had the motive, the opportunity, and the means to commit the crime with which he or she is charged. These are the links in the chain that can shackle a defendant, but the chain can be no stronger than its weakest link. For Paul the weakest link was motive, which indeed was nonexistent: the prosecution could give no reason at all for the shooting. On this matter the jurors could only speculate, which they were undoubtedly cautioned against doing time and again. But in the absence of a piece of vital information, many jurors will feel a need to go searching for it if only in their own minds. This is precisely what speculation is. Among Paul's jurors speculation proved fruitless, but what caused it—the prosecution's failure to offer a motive for the crime—saved the defendant from conviction on the more serious charges and, given all the other circumstances, made a compromise verdict inevitable.

The Case of the Hidden Medicine

The last jury room we will visit bristles with tension from the moment the jurors file in to start their deliberations. The defendant, Tom Brooks, has been indicted for first-degree murder in a state where that crime is punishable by death. Brooks, accused of having slain the owner of a grocery store during the course of a robbery, has confessed to the killing, but his attorney has argued that mitigating circumstances make Brooks innocent of the crime charged. If he is found guilty there is a good chance that he will be sentenced to die in the electric chair.

The trial has dragged on for almost a month and the jurors, although they have not been sequestered, have come to know one another on a first-name basis. We begin just after they have elected their foreman in a unanimous vote:

Foreman: I'm not sure I should be grateful for this honor. I can't help thinking all the rest of you are just too chicken to get up in court and condemn a man to death.

Brad: The judge will do that. All you'll have to say is "guilty."

Foreman: There's a distinction without a difference. (After a long silence) Well, doesn't anybody want to say anything?

Ken: What is there to say? Brooks is a confessed killer.

Colin: It's his first offense.

Ken: So? Are we supposed to let him go free so he can commit a second?

Foreman: I'm sure no one here wants him to go free.

Pete: Hell, no. The question is do we want him to fry. And I say yes.

Foreman: Nicely put, Pete. Suppose we take a vote on whether or not we want Tom Brooks to fry.

Pamela: No. Not yet. Let's talk first.

Colin: I'm not prepared to vote either.

Clare: Nor am I. If you insist on voting now, I'll pass.

Pete: What goes on here? I don't think I understand you people. Didn't you hear what I heard these last four weeks? This punk killed a seventy-year-old man in cold blood. He got up on the stand, and he told us he did it—shot him not once, not twice, not three times, but four times. Four times, friends.

Colin: He only hit him twice.

Pete: Man, are you for real? That guy, Genovese, is dead— D–E–A–D—dead. What the hell does it matter how many bullets went into his gut? Just one was enough to finish him.

Foreman: Calm down, Pete.

Pete: Whadya mean, calm down. I'm losing four weeks pay sitting on this jury, and I want to get the damn thing over with.

Clare: We've all lost something by being here, but that shouldn't make us rush into a decision.

Pete: With all due respect, honey, you don't work for a living. You can afford to spend another couple of days jabbering around this table here. I can't. (To the foreman) C'mon, let's take a vote.

Foreman: Pete, our verdict has to be unanimous, correct?

Pete: Yeah, so?

Foreman: So if at least three people refuse to vote, what will we have accomplished? We might as well talk now as later.

Brad: I agree with Clare—we shouldn't be hasty—but I also agree with Pete—what in God's name is there to talk about? Brooks is a *confessed* killer. He's guilty.

Stanford (to the foreman): Bill, if you'll permit me. Can I ask for a show of hands? Does anyone think Brooks is not guilty?

Pamela: Of what?

Pete: Of what? I must be dreaming. Of what? Of murder, for Christ's sake!

Stanford: Yes, of murder.

Pamela: Of first-degree murder? If you're asking for a show of hands on that, I pass.

Pete (rising from his seat): And I give up.

Foreman: We've only started, Pete. Sit down. Obviously, the problem we face is in the crime Brooks is charged with. I'm certain that no one here doubts that he shot and killed Arnold Genovese.

Pete (sitting down): From what I been hearing the last five minutes, I'm not so sure.

Foreman: Does anyone doubt that? (Silence—a few people shake their heads.)

Pete: Hallelujah.

Foreman: So the question is of what crime do we convict the defendant.

Stanford: And we *can* find him guilty of manslaughter.

Pete: Brooks? That punk? After what he done? That'd be like giving him a traffic ticket.

Foreman: The fact is the judge did offer us that option.

Stanford: And if we believe Brooks shot Genovese without premeditation, that's exactly how we should vote.

Ken: Well, let me say that I was confused when the judge gave us that option. I thought—

Pete (interrupting): Man, she didn't mean it. She didn't mean it, friends. It must be the law or something that she had to say that. Did you see her face when she talked about manslaughter? Using all those hundred-dollar words. "Premeditation." "Malice aforethought." Bull. That's bull. She said those words like they smelled bad.

Brad: Y'know, Pete's right.

Pete: 'Course I'm right.

Brad: She did talk about manslaughter as if the very idea of it was distasteful to her.

Pamela: The idea of the electric chair is distasteful to me.

Pete: Honey, I promise you'll never get near one.

Ken: Please let me go on. I don't care whether the judge wants us to vote for manslaughter or not. I'll vote the way I want to vote. But I thought that murder committed when you're trying to rob somebody can't be anything but murder. I can't see how there can be even a possibility of manslaughter.

Stanford: There is if there was no premeditation.

Ken: But that's my point. There had to be premeditation, as I see it.

Pete: Ken, you are so right.

Ken: Let me review the crime for a minute. Just to help me explain my point. It's ten o'clock in the morning. A grocery store on the outskirts of town. No one around. It snowed all day the day before. And because Genovese couldn't get to the bank in the afternoon, there is more money than usual in the till. He lives with his wife above the store. He comes downstairs, unlocks the front door—

Pete (interrupting): Ken, I love you, but is this trip necessary?

Ken: Be patient. I'll get to my point in a second. I'm just

setting the scene. Anyway, Genovese unlocks the door and starts back toward the counter. He is about ten feet away from it when Tom Brooks walks in. He was obviously hiding just out of sight, waiting for Genovese to open up.

Colin: We can't be sure of that—about his hiding, I mean. He denied—

Pete (interrupting): What the hell's the difference if he was hiding or not?

Foreman: Colin, you do accept the fact that Tom Brooks entered the store seconds after Genovese unlocked the door. Mrs. Genovese testified that he went downstairs at—

Colin (interrupting): Nine fifty-nine, I know. It's the hiding part that bothered me. We have only the district attorney's word for that and—

Ken (interrupting): True but not important. Let me go on. Brooks enters the store. Genovese turns around immediately— and this is Brooks's own testimony, don't forget—and he's standing there with a gun aimed right at Genovese's chest. The old man doesn't say a word. He's struck dumb, speechless. We all agree? (Everyone either nods or says yes.) We have to agree because Brooks testified to that, and he's the only one who was there.

Pamela: And you don't think he's lying?

Ken: About this? Of course not. Anyway, Brooks says, "Give me all your cash." Genovese still doesn't say anything. He doesn't move either. He's rooted to the spot, staring down a gun barrel. Brooks says, "C'mon, move it. I ain't got all day." Still Genovese says nothing. Finally he turns around and starts walking very slowly toward the counter. He turns back once, as if he's going to say something. But he doesn't—he doesn't say a word. He goes behind the counter. The cash register's right there. He stoops—

Pamela (interrupting): You're leaving something out. It was when Genovese turned and Brooks thought he was going to speak that Brooks said, "Look, Pop, I don't want to hurt you. I—"

Pete (interrupting): Wrong, honey. He said that when he first came in, as soon as Genovese looked around and saw him.

Pamela: Sorry, Pete, but I'm afraid you're wrong. And I'd appreciate it if you didn't call me honey.

Ken: Is it really that important when Brooks said it? Can't I finish before we talk about that?

Pamela: It's terribly important to me. But by all means finish.

Ken: Thank you. Genovese stoops. He's not opening the cash register. He's getting something from under the counter. Brooks yells, "What the hell you doing?" Genovese doesn't answer. He's trying to reach his heart medicine, but since he can't speak, he can't tell Brooks that. Brooks yells, "Don't try anything, Pop. Stand up." But Genovese is still bent down trying to find that little bottle of pills under the cash register. Brooks walks behind the counter, sees Genovese reaching for something on the shelf just below the register. Brooks yells out again, "Stand up." Genovese doesn't. So Brooks plugs him—four bullets, fast, one right after the other. Two go into the floor, one into Genovese's arm, one into his chest. Then Brooks steps over the bloody body, unlocks the cash register, scoops out eight hundred and forty-two bucks and hotfoots it out of the store. (Pausing) Now just about everything I just said comes from Brooks's own story on the stand, right? (Everyone either nods or voices agreement.) Well then, can someone point out to me one thing—just one thing— that Brooks did that wasn't completely intentional?

Colin: You use the word "intentional." Of course, Brooks didn't do anything *by* accident—

Ken (interrupting): Exactly. He walked into the store intending to rob it. He ordered Genovese at gunpoint to hand over his cash. And he shot the old man—who was in the middle of having a heart attack—because he wasn't moving fast enough.

Pamela: No, that's not so. He shot Genovese because he thought he was reaching for a weapon.

Clare: He even said he didn't want to shoot him.

Pete: And you believe that punk? You think he'd leave Genovese to finger him in a lineup someday? Oh, honey, grow up.

Foreman: Pete, may I suggest you stop addressing the women on the jury as "honey."

Pete: Would they prefer "birdbrain"?

Pamela: No, Pete, we wouldn't. Particularly coming from you. You're all wrong about the time Brooks said, "I don't want to hurt you."

Pete: Whaddaya talking about? Brooks said it when he walked in. These punks all say it right at the beginning—(speaking very slowly)—to trick their victims into cooperating, get it? To hand over the cash fast. If the poor sucker thinks he has a chance he gives the punk the dough and hopes he'll leave. Sometimes the punk even obliges and sometimes, like Brooks, he don't.

Clare: Very interesting. You obviously know a lot about these things, Pete. But Pam is right—*Brooks* made that statement later, when Genovese stopped on his way to the cash register.

Pamela: It was when he thought Genovese might put up some resistance, and that's *why* he said, "I don't want to hurt you."

Ken: Aha, now I get it. You two ladies are saying that Brooks made the statement for good reason—that he really meant it. And Pete is saying that for Brooks, it was kind of automatic, that it meant nothing, really.

Stanford: And if Brooks said it when he first walked in, Pete would be right. Genovese was certainly not indicating any resistance at that point.

Foreman: So the time the statement was made becomes very important.

Pete: Take my word for it. He said it when he walked in: "I don't wanna hurt you. Gimme all your cash and—"

Clare: Pete, you're making that up! Brooks never put those two sentences together in that way.

Foreman: Let's not argue. Let's find out. We'll go back into the courtroom and have Brooks's testimony read back to us. I'll ring for the bailiff.

The jury returns to the courtroom. The judge, having received the foreman's written request, directs the court stenographer to read aloud a substantial portion of the defendant's testimony that includes the statement at issue. Pamela and Clare prove to be right: Brooks testified that when he entered the grocery store he said only, "This is it, Pop. Give me all your cash, and fast." It was later, when Genovese, walking toward the cash register, stopped and turned around, that Brooks said, "I don't want to hurt you, Pop. Just keep moving and do what I say and you'll be all right."

The jurors are back in the jury room:

Pete: Well, that wasted another half hour.

Stanford: Wasted?

Pete: Yeah, wasted. What the hell difference does it make when he said it? For one thing, we have only Brooks's word that he said it at all. And for another thing, dammit, whenever the hell he said it, he didn't mean it. He killed the guy, right? We all agree on that, even the bleeding hearts. So how could he mean it when he said, "I don't want to hurt you?"

Stanford: He could have meant it when he said it. But when he thought Genovese was trying to find a gun, he got scared and shot him.

Brad: So you're buying precisely what Brooks's lawyer is trying to sell.

Foreman: That, of course, is his whole case.

Colin: That and the fact that Tom was never in trouble before.

Ken: He's only twenty years old. Give him time. He may never have committed a crime before, but he hasn't accomplished anything either. A high school dropout who hasn't held a job for more than two weeks.

Clare: No father, a mother who's never home.

Pete: Whadya mean a mother who's never home? She's out working to support this punk.

Brad: It seems to me we are straying from the issue.

Pamela: No we're not, Brad. The issue is the life of a twenty-year-old boy.

Brad: For you, perhaps. As I understood the judge, we have only to determine whether Tom Brooks deliberately and with premeditation murdered Arnold Genovese while attempting to rob him, which is also a Class A felony.

Pete: Hey, that's good. Did you memorize all that? That's great. You oughta go to law school.

Foreman: Pamela and Brad are both right, or each one is half right. Together, what you're saying is that we must decide whether this defendant committed the crime as charged, realizing that if we do so decide, he may very well be electrocuted.

Ken: True, very true. And I've come to a conclusion. Even if Brooks fired his gun only when he thought Genovese was going to resist, even if he had no intention of shooting before that moment, there was still premeditation. He wanted to shoot that gun. For whatever reason *he felt he had to shoot that gun.*

Pete: Right on, man.

Pamela: But the reason matters.

Ken: I don't see that it does. The very fact that Brooks was in that shop for the purpose of committing a felony makes any reason he had—just as long as he had a reason and didn't shoot by accident—proof of premeditation.

Stanford: But the reason may spell the difference between murder and manslaughter.

Brad: Why do you keep bringing up manslaughter when that verdict would force us to go beyond the evidence we have and try to dig into this boy's mind? We can't do that very easily, we don't have to, and the judge herself at least implied that she didn't want us to. Why can't we just weigh the evidence that is incontrovertible?

Foreman: In other words, why can't we read Tom's thoughts from his actions?

Brad: Exactly.

Clare (to the foreman): To answer your question, Bill, because that way, in all likelihood, we would convict him of first-degree murder.

Pamela: And I won't do that. I refuse to be in any way responsible for sending this boy to his death.

Foreman: Pam, let me ask you—if there were no chance that he'd fry, as Pete would say—if there were no capital punishment in this state, would you be prepared to find Tom Brooks guilty of murder?

Pamela (after a long pause): I suppose so.

Clare: But there is capital punishment.

Pete: Well, can ya beat that? Capital punishment is gonna keep this punk alive.

Ken: Pete, you're not going to like this, but may I suggest that we go back to the courtroom and ask the judge to spell out more clearly the differences between murder and manslaughter.

Pete: I'll tell ya the difference—with one of them we get rid of the punk for good, and with the other he's back on the street in a few years, bumping off another poor slob.

Ken: It's really "premeditation" that I want more fully explained, and I don't think even you can help me out with that.

Again the jurors return to the courtroom. At their request the judge carefully explains that in this case "premeditation" would mean Tom Brooks had made a deliberate decision to kill Arnold Genovese before he pulled the fatal trigger. The judge goes on to clarify the basis on which the jury could find for manslaughter: if Tom Brooks had fired in a moment of panic or extreme fear or if he had thought his own life was in danger.

As soon as the jury resumes its deliberations, Ken announces that somewhat reluctantly he now favors a manslaughter verdict; he does not believe beyond a reasonable doubt that Brooks wanted to kill Genovese. Before too long, all the jurors agree to the lesser charge except Pete, who thus becomes—and for hours remains—a lone holdout. By eight P.M., the foreman reports that the jury is hopelessly deadlocked, but the judge, refusing to declare a mistrial, orders the jurors to resume deliberations in the morning and sequesters them for the night.

When they reassemble in the jury room the next day, Pete, under a barrage of pleas and questions, admits that he is certain Brooks is a vicious killer—not primarily because of anything that was brought out during the trial, but because Brooks reminds him of other murderers he has read about and one whom he knew personally. Armed with this new fact, the other jurors attack Pete for basing his verdict on circumstances that he cannot prove to be truly relevant. Says the foreman, "Every person is an individual, and Tom Brooks may not be anything like these other men you remember." Pete, saying that he is "fed up" with

all of them and with this case, at last gives in. He'll vote for manslaughter just so that he can get back to work.

As the jurors in Tom Brooks's case began their deliberations, they enjoyed an advantage that was not given to our other four juries: a confession from the defendant. But, less fortunately, they were also unique in knowing that their verdict could possibly send a man to his death. These two factors played against one another, forcing the jury to examine and weigh the confession —which was obviously the most important piece of evidence offered during the trial—in a very special light. Let's consider exactly what happened.

First of all we should note that, surprisingly, given the powerfully damaging nature of Tom Brooks's confession, a few jurors seemed to show a fastidious concern for minor details of the crime: the number of bullets shot versus the number that hit their target; whether or not the defendant was hiding before he entered the grocery store; and, most important, exactly when Brooks said, "I don't want to hurt you." If, for reasons we will discuss in a moment, some jurors are fearful of where the "big" facts lead, they will make every effort to follow the "little" facts, in hope that they will bring the jury to a less terrible destination.

Second, among any group of jurors there is often at least one person with a methodical mind who will systematically and exhaustively review the evidence. In a sense, the person is thinking out loud, in order to answer either his or her own questions or those of others. On this jury, Ken was such a person; his deliberate reconstruction of the crime served to uncover a significant disagreement about the facts, while his determination to understand thoroughly the options the jurors had been given resulted in the eventual verdict.

Third, in situations marked by stress and conflict, jurors welcome a return to the courtroom. Of course, there is usually a sound, practical reason for their trip, whether it be on clarification of a matter of evidence or for judicial guidance for possible verdicts. But the less obvious benefits of providing a break in the tension and an opportunity to reconsider should not be overlooked. In the Tom Brooks trial, the jury's second return to the courtroom cleared the air and enabled Ken to make the crucial change in his thinking.

Fourth, while it is the jury's recognized responsibility only to determine the facts of a case, quite frequently jurors refuse to stop there. As in the Case of Nathaniel Trueblood, a few jurors in the Case of the Hidden Medicine focused on the difference between facts and values. The facts seemed to spell doom for Tom Brooks, but looking beyond them to their own values, these jurors would not consent to a decision that invited the denial of life.

The attitudes expressed or implied by Colin, Pam, Stanford, and Clare are not at all uncommon among jurors who know their verdict may lead to the death penalty. A discussion of the highly controversial issue of capital punishment is beyond the scope of this book. It must be said, however, that even those who claim to favor capital punishment in the abstract, often resist being a party to it when for them the abstract becomes real. Observers disagree violently about whether the death penalty acts as a deterrent to crime, but there can be no dispute about whether it acts as a deterrent to conviction. Study after study has shown that jurors are reluctant to find a defendant guilty when such a verdict could result in his execution. Thus, to paraphrase Pete, capital punishment has kept some punks alive.

*   *   *

In one important sense every jury is sequestered: for as long as it takes them to reach a verdict, the twelve people are imprisoned in a room that is totally cut off from the outside world. Deprived of the contacts, relationships, and activities that give substance to their everyday lives, they are forced to create together a new, if temporary, world, one in which they are the only inhabitants, twelve chairs and a table the only furnishings, and blank walls the only landscape. But into this world rush all sorts of invisible agents—the experiences, perceptions, and attitudes accumulated over a dozen disparate lifetimes and a comparatively few shared hours. It is impossible to predict how these varying factors will clash or correspond, what sparks will be struck, which paths will converge. In the small world of the jury room the possibilities of conflict, compromise, and accommodation are as infinite as are the ways of human behavior in the world outside the courthouse.

We have tried in this chapter to identify and illustrate some principles and practices that are common to jury deliberations. If space allowed we could have analyzed jury deliberations in trial after trial, reducing hours of discussion and debate to a handful of key developments, isolating the people and the pronouncements that, seen in retrospect, hastened the trend or turned the tide toward one verdict or another. But all our knowledge of the past can give us no certainty for the future, for every jury creates a new world of its own. Listen to a man who has just rejoined the world outside:

I knew the defendant was guilty but I didn't know how or why I knew. I sensed it, that's all; I sensed it. The lawyers were no help at all. You wouldn't believe how unevenly matched they were. If they'd been in a boxing ring, the referee would have stopped the fight a minute into the first round. The D.A. was a total incompetent. I guess he was inexperienced—he seemed pretty young—and he was almost inarticulate. He kept repeating himself and missing opportunities to make points. He didn't even try to build up the testimony that could have helped him, and he was like struck dumb and powerless against the witnesses who hurt him. I'm sure you can tell I've served on juries before and let me say this guy was the pits—the absolute bottom.

To make matters worse, he was up against a defense attorney who was spectacular—really, a legal virtuoso. Of course, there was no way he could prove this guy was innocent but that's not the name of the game anyhow. He just ripped the state's case to shreds. The D.A.'s expert witnesses left the stand looking like embarrassed amateurs. The eyewitnesses might just as well have been blind when that lawyer got through with them. I'm telling you, when the D.A. rested his case, it was like burying a bunch of dust. Unbelievable. But still I *knew* the guy was guilty. I *sensed* that he was guilty. But convincing the other jurors of that—forget it.

There was one woman who agreed with me, and it was the

two of us against the mob. Almost from the moment we walked in the jury room, and certainly after the first vote, the ten of them were shouting at us to explain why we wanted to convict and, dammit, we had no answer. And they would trot out this argument and that argument and all I could say was, "The lawyer made you see it that way. He twisted the testimony around." And then all of a sudden I remembered. It must have been lodged in my unconscious all the time and that's why I sensed he was guilty. Nothing to do with any witnesses or testimony or evidence or lawyers or judge. Nothing to do with any prejudices or even gut feelings. I was just sitting there picturing the defendant and then it hit me. There was never a moment when two armed cops weren't standing next to him.

I've served on three criminal cases—one of them for murder —and I never saw that before. This guy was up for armed robbery. Why did he need that honor guard? I asked the ten jurors that. About half of them had served on a criminal case before and they all admitted that they'd never seen a defendant guarded that way. Well, that broke the ice. We all started to see through the lawyer's tactics. It took a while but we convicted. Afterwards we found out that the guy was an escaped con, serving a term for manslaughter. That's why he had those cops with him all the time: his own personal cops. They never said a word but they nailed him all right.

PENALTIES

What Jurors May Expect

When Their Verdict Is Delivered

and After the Trial Is Over

After the moment of decision comes the moment of highest drama. Although the announcement of a jury's verdict seldom provokes the kind of pandemonium that it did in the Lizzie Borden case, it almost always triggers the release of deep and conflicting emotions and brings to an end a period of mounting suspense. In the courtroom, the tension begins to rise as soon as the jury retires to deliberate; in the halls outside the courtroom, in the lawyers' offices, and in the holding cell where (if not out on bail) the defendant waits, it increases for as long as the jury is out; it reaches its crest in the courtroom when the jurors, having reported that they have reached agreement, are returned to the jury box.

The attorneys, the witnesses, and the judge have all had "their day in court." Now it is the jurors' turn to command center stage. All eyes are upon them as their foreman is asked, first, if they have reached a verdict, and then, what that verdict is.

The foreman's response is an expression of judgment that can itself be judged in many ways. On the level of drama, the verdict is always effective for it serves as both climax and conclusion to all that has gone before. In terms of its immediate human consequences, the verdict may produce elation or disappointment for the defendant and those close to him, for the opposing attorneys, and for many of the spectators—including perhaps the victim of the crime or his survivors. In terms of its broader social impact, the verdict is most likely to be ignored, but it may bring great satisfaction to a community, or, as has been known to happen, it may ignite a rage so uncontainable that it soon bursts into violence. In terms of its legal correctness, the verdict, if it is guilty, may later be either upheld or overturned by a higher court.

But whatever the emotions a verdict generates, and whatever the events that, in the near or distant future, follow from it, that instant when, with the defendant facing him, the foreman pronounces the words "guilty" or "not guilty" has a symbolic value that stands apart from all other considerations: it marks the attempt of sadly imperfect men and women, in circumstances of stress, conflict, and challenge, to deal with each other fairly and rationally. It is, in short, proof that we are at least trying to be civilized.

When jurors deliver a not-guilty verdict, they have shut a final door on the case, shut it and sealed it forever. The constitutional ban on double jeopardy assures a defendant that he will never again have to answer to charges of which he has just been acquitted. Assuming that he has not been, or will not be, accused of other related crimes on which he has yet to be tried (if he has, this not-guilty verdict in itself does not offset the other charges), the defendant is now free to leave the courtroom and, indeed, free to try to live his life as if he had never been forced to stand trial. His success in doing so may well depend on how highly publicized his trial was. If it was largely ignored, as most trials are, it is only his memories of it that may continue to haunt him.

There is no such finality in a verdict of guilty. If, as the title of the first chapter of this book suggests, a verdict is the end of a story, a guilty verdict is very often also the beginning of another. To avoid condemnation of the innocent and to insure the rights of the guilty, our legal system provides defendants with a series of safeguards—mechanisms and opportunities for them to demonstrate that a conviction is unfair, baseless, unlawful—in a word, wrong. While the appeal of a conviction to the United States Supreme Court, years after the defendant's trial, would be the last of the available safeguards, a practice known as *polling the jury* is the first.

Polling the Jury

It takes place minutes after the verdict of guilty has been announced. The defense attorney may move that the jurors be asked individually whether they support the verdict. The judge invariably grants the motion, and the ritual that follows is as eerie and relentless as a bell tolling midnight: twelve different voices repeating, in turn, the word "guilty," truly a chorus of doom.

Why, you may well ask, do defense attorneys bother? What end do they hope to accomplish? Their clients certainly cannot enjoy hearing a knell-like judgment against them echo and re-echo in the chamber, and surely a jury would never announce agreement on a verdict unless its twelve members had in fact achieved unanimity.

Let us return for a moment to Mrs. Jackson in The Case of the Missing Motive. Remember her reluctance to find the defendant guilty of *any* charge. Imagine the inner conflicts she had to resolve before she could go along with her fellow jurors. Now, let us suppose Mrs. Jackson has a son who is about Paul's age or a sister whom she has come to distrust and despise, or perhaps a memory of a time when she herself accused someone unjustly and feelings of remorse that have plagued her ever since. Now put her in the jury box, force her to look upon Paul as he sits condemned at the defense table, and ask her finally to pronounce aloud, like a curse, the word "guilty." It is not beyond the realm of possibility that, no longer subject to the pressures that assailed her in the jury room, and with only her own conscience to answer to, she will reverse her decision and prolong the deliberation or cause a mistrial.

Jurors are polled because they *have* been known to change their minds. Not long ago just such a turnabout occurred in a small Southern city. A jury had found a defendant guilty of murder and, subsequently, in a procedure we will discuss below, voted to condemn him to death. When the foreman announced that the jury had unanimously agreed to sentence him to the gas chamber, the defendant fainted, toppling over in his chair. His attorney immediately moved to have the jurors polled. The defendant had regained consciousness by the time the judge reached the seventh juror. Did she support the death sentence, he asked. For a moment she was silent, and then softly she replied, "No." Amid general dismay and confusion the jurors were sent back to the jury room to reconsider their sentence. They never again reached agreement, and since in that state the death penalty can be imposed only by unanimous verdict, the judge was eventually forced to sentence the defendant, a thirty-year-old man convicted of strangling a ninety-year-old woman, to imprisonment for life.

Perhaps the classic justification for polling the jury was expressed most tersely in a recent trial in New York City. After many hours of deliberation, the jury had found for conviction, but when polling reached the tenth juror, he jumped to his feet and shouted, "Not guilty!" Then, before anyone in the courtroom could react to his thunderbolt, in full voice he went on: "You beat me down in there—but you can't beat me down out here!"

Passing Sentence

In the same city five months later, the longest criminal trial in the state's history came to a close as a jury found four defendants guilty of murder. They had deliberated for two and a half days, which seems no more than the wink of an eye when compared to the year, three months, and three days that the rest of the trial consumed. But after they reached their verdict, the jurors were at last free to go home, their obligations fully and honorably discharged. If they had been serving in North Carolina, however, or one of the other thirteen states—mainly in the South—that require juries to pass sentence on those they have convicted of capital crimes (that is, crimes punishable by death), the jurors would have had to return to the jury room with a new set of instructions from the judge. Instead of a simple guilty or not-guilty verdict, the options now offered to them would include the full range of sentences that the state has determined may be appropriate for someone convicted of murder. Now, too, information would be given to the jury that may have been deliberately withheld earlier: a profile of the defendant that includes, most significantly, his prior criminal record—if any.

In determining sentences, such matters as the evidence presented in court and the past history and character of the defendant must now be viewed from a different perspective, one that will, it is hoped, yield eventual agreement not on *whether* the defendant committed the crime but on *how* and *why* he came to commit it. If the jury finally decides that his act was heartless, cold-blooded, brutal, savage, or any other adjective that suggests deliberate and inhuman cruelty, they will surely impose the harshest penalty available to them. Conversely, if the jury decides that the crime was touched by mitigating circumstances—excessive pressures on the defendant, from without or within, that he was not fully responsible for, emotions that were momentarily uncontrollable—they will in all likelihood show leniency and may even opt for the lightest possible penalty. Between the two extremes lie other choices, and, of course, the chance that the jurors will fail to reach any agreement at all on punishment.

They begin with the advantage of their unanimous belief in the defendant's guilt, but this may be more than offset by their physical or mental weariness and by their obligation to explore and understand more deeply than before the tangled web that is the defendant's psyche. Thus, insofar as they are required to determine not merely the fact of guilt but the *degree* of guilt—just how bad a person this criminal is and how severely he should be punished—those who must impose sentence are perhaps faced with the most formidable demands made of any jurors anywhere.

The Aftermath of the Trial

In most states, however, sentencing isn't required of the jury, and when the twelfth juror has been polled and has expressed agreement with the announced decision, the trial is virtually over. True, a guilty verdict will probably prompt the defense attorney to inform the court that he intends to file certain motions, and the judge will, of course, have to set a date for sentencing. These are but the closing movements in a ritual whose end is always the same: the judge will turn his attention to the twelve people in the jury box, thank them for their services, and perhaps answer any questions they may have.

All at once the untold story of the trial (untold, that is, to the jury) may unfold. At last the jurors learn of the balky witness who disappeared just before she was due to take the stand, or of behind-the-scenes legal maneuvering that almost succeeded in halting the trial days earlier, or of defense charges that the defendant's rights were being violated. The court would have considered any and all such developments potentially prejudicial to the jury's thinking had they been divulged in the course of the trial. Only now can they be spoken of in open court and now, of course, even if this new information dramatically changes a juror's opinion, it is too late to change the verdict. The court is adjourned.

Back home the jurors will probably have to wait a few weeks to receive the modest payment the state provides for their services, but they are probably free to talk about their experiences immediately. A not uncommon myth has it that jury room deliberations are to remain forever secret, sacred, and inviolate. Don't you believe it. While jurors are not permitted to speak of a trial *while it is in progress,* once it is over they may freely do so unless the judge has specifically directed otherwise. In a living room or on a bus, at a dinner party or during a coffee break, they may bore or enthrall their companions with as many of the details of the trial as they can recall, including quite decidedly whatever went on in the jury room.

At the end of a much publicized trial, jurors are likely to be besieged by the press, peppered with questions and requests for interviews. The reporters are merely doing their job; jurors may respond in whatever way they wish. Reveling in the attention, they may hold court on their own and, if their audience will listen for that long, explain in three hours why the jury was out for only two. Or, clamlike, they may make a tight-lipped dash to their cars, and once home, lock their doors behind them, pull down their shades, and refuse to answer phone calls. They are compelled neither to speak nor to remain silent. In the days, weeks, and months that follow, they may write a book about the trial (though they must be careful of the libel laws if they commit to print descriptions of their fellow jurors), they may be guests on television talk shows, or they may fly to Nepal to live among the Sherpas until all the excitement has quieted down.

It may, however, be a long time before a trial is forgotten; indeed, like Lizzie Borden's, it may be remembered for centuries. Sometimes there is good reason for jurors to reclaim public attention. Not long ago, two days after a front-page trial had ended with a hung jury, jurors regained headlines by informing the press that their lone holdout had made remarks during deliberations that strongly suggested he was privy to information about the crime that had never been presented in court. In the late 1960s, in a case referred to earlier, jurors revealed, long after they had convicted a defendant of murder, that during the trial period some of their group had paid a secret midnight visit to the scene of the crime. Both of these rather electrifying disclosures had serious and immediate consequences; in the first case, the district attorney's office began an investigation into the possibility of jury tampering; in the second, the conviction was reversed and a new trial ordered.

But jurors who make posttrial statements usually do so to far less effect. Recently, a jury got together weeks after acquitting a physician of mass murder and released a statement to the press demanding that the doctor's license be reinstated so that he could resume his medical practice. This was shortly before jurors in another case asked that they be allowed to change their month-old verdict of guilty of criminally negligent homicide to not guilty of anything because, to their dismay, the convicted man had been handed a far more severe sentence than they had expected. Both of these juries succeeded in getting themselves back into the newspapers, but they accomplished nothing else.

Generally, however, if jurors receive or are restored to public attention sometime after a trial is over, it is due to actions other than their own. Since felony convictions almost always lead to appeals, long-forgotten juries may years later again be in the news when a higher court decides, for example, that they were unfairly chosen or improperly instructed by the judge or inade-quately sequestered. Ironically, the great majority of higher court rulings that create headlines concern cases that went totally unnoticed by the press when they were originally tried. So a decision on appeal, if it relates in some way to the jury in the case at issue, may bring belated recognition to twelve people whose service had been lost to all but courthouse records and their own memories.

The fact is, of course, that most jurors cherish their anonymity; when their service is over they want nothing more than to return to their homes, their jobs, and their everyday lives. A court of law is not their normal habitat, and they probably will not mind if they never again are required to enter one. But every juror lives in a community, and a community cannot be ignored. Un-like a courthouse with its strict rules and limited demands, a community can act in ways that are unexpected, random, fright-ening, and destructive. And it is a community that can exact from a juror a penalty that is far more severe than the hours of boredom, the lost paychecks, the unwelcome conflict, and the missed vacation that jury duty may impose.

Unpopular verdicts have led to mass demonstrations, to violence in the streets, to destruction of property and injury of people. Those who riot probably never entered the courtroom, and they certainly did not see and hear the case exactly as the jury did. They may know more or less than the jurors, but, regardless, what propels them to act is not their knowledge but their sympathy. It may be for a defendant whom they feel was unfairly convicted or, more likely in our time, for a victim whom they consider insufficiently avenged—or, if the defendant was acquitted, not avenged at all. The jurors whose decision caused the havoc are rarely in any personal danger—mob action is not directed or knowing or sensible enough to proceed against twelve different targets. But as they consider the results of what they have done, how can the jurors not wonder at the way men and women make a mockery of their own system of justice?

Fortunately for us, this kind of reaction to an unpopular verdict is today an uncommon—indeed, an extraordinary—event. But when it does occur, it throws into sharp relief the passions and the irrationality that laws and courts and juries are intended to control. It may be small comfort to jurors who feel abused and maligned, but, like all jurors, they should recognize that they have met a need that is essential to the well-being of the community. Whatever the aftermath of a trial may be, jurors should in time look back upon their service as a contribution to the public good, and, it is to be hoped, as an experience that stretched their minds—taught them something of how our legal system works, broadened their understanding of others, and perhaps even deepened their knowledge of themselves.

"TWELVE PEOPLE OF AVERAGE IGNORANCE"

The Jury System on Trial

"Ladies and gentlemen, have you reached a verdict?"

"We have."

"What is your verdict?"

"We find the jury system guilty of undemocratic practices and gross inefficiencies. In general, it falls far short of the goals it is intended to achieve."

Such a harsh judgment of the jury system would be expressed today not by a randomly chosen group of twelve people but by thousands of men and women who have participated in or observed jury trials and by thousands more who have given extensive study to the jury system as a crucial aspect of our legal structure. What these critics find so troubling is certainly not the concept of the laymen jury—they are fierce champions of that—but many of the ways in which the jury system actually operates in courtrooms throughout the United States.

In this chapter we will be begin by examining the major charges leveled by these critics, along with the measures, often controversial in themselves, that have been taken to eliminate the shortcomings. We will then consider the views of a much smaller group of critics, those who believe that the very idea of a laymen jury, however effectively it may be implemented, is fundamentally unsound and should be consigned to oblivion. We will conclude by responding to this sweeping attack, in our case for the defense emphasizing those strengths of the jury system that are, ultimately, the source of its survival.

* * *

The ideal of the jury system in criminal trials can be stated quite simply: a person or persons accused of wrongdoing is judged by a sizable group of his peers, people who are truly representative of the public at large and who are open-minded, impartial, wise, willing, and attentive. Between this ideal and the reality that can be observed every day in our courtrooms stretches a chasm that is hard to defend and harder still to narrow. Critics find weaknesses in the way jurors are chosen, the way they are treated, the way they function. Perhaps the most widespread and certainly the most explosive of their charges concerns the underrepresentation on juries of minority groups.

Imbalances in Representation

It is the right of every man accused of any offense to be tried by a jury of his peers. I claim that the black man is my peer, and so I am not tried by my peers unless there be one or more black men in the jury box.

So spoke the Reverend J. W. Hood at a convention of freedmen in North Carolina in 1865, the year the Civil War ended and three years after Emancipation was proclaimed. If he were restored to life today, the reverend would have good reason to repeat his statement.

Consider these findings for some typical city and statewide federal courts in 1974:

City	% of Nonwhites* in Population**	% of Nonwhites on Juries	Discrepancy in %
Atlanta, Ga.	18.4	15.3	− 16.8
Camden, N.J.	11.0	7.8	− 29.1
Denver, Colo.	4.3	2.7	− 37.2
Hartford, Conn.	4.6	2.5	− 45.7
San Francisco, Ca.	14.1	10.0	− 29.1
Tampa, Fla.	8.5	5.7	− 32.9
State			
Delaware	13.2	12.7	− 3.8
Maryland	16.7	11.0	− 34.1
New Mexico	8.3	0	−100.

*Includes Blacks, Orientals, and Native Americans
**From 1970 census

Granted that the statistics may have improved in the years since the mid-70s. Granted, too, that the representation of nonwhites on juries is much greater in such heavily urban areas as New York City, Newark, and Detroit than it is elsewhere. Granted, finally, that over the years the Supreme Court has consistently and deliberately refrained from setting strict guidelines as to the percentage of minority groups that must be represented in jury pools. Nevertheless, no one can dispute the fact that in most

localities—and nonwhite representation on state court juries is generally below that on federal court juries—members of racial minorities are sitting in the jury box in proportions that do not even approach their numbers in the community. You need no survey to prove that; just go into a courtroom and look.

The causes of this have their roots in the means used to select people for the jury pool. Most jurisdictions employ voter lists. Some sixteen states, mostly in New England and the South, allow local officials to pick and choose names from these lists; in other states, jurors are selected from them randomly. When prospective jurors are chosen by civic or political leaders, it is quite probable that middle-aged, middle-class white men will dominate the so-called "cross section of the community." But even when selection is at random, by making registration to vote in effect a prerequisite to jury service, we are decisively excluding a large part of any population.

It may be a national disgrace that so many millions of Americans choose not to register for presidential elections, but individually any number of them may have good reason for "sitting it out." They may simply be discouraged by the cumbersome and haphazard voter registration procedures that prevail in so many states. And even if their motives are less than compelling— perhaps they feel removed from the mainstream of political life, perhaps they are disenchanted with the candidates—nonvoters still represent a substantial segment of the community. By keeping them out of the jury pool we insure the underrepresentation of those groups that traditionally go to the polls in the smallest numbers: racial minorities, the young, and the elderly.

To make the jury pool more representative, some states have acted to supplement the voter lists—using census information where it is available, Social Security records, income tax returns, and lists of those who hold drivers' licenses, among other sources. Indeed, in the decade of the 70s, spurred largely by Supreme Court rulings, more was done to correct imbalances in the jury pool than was even attempted in other areas considered ripe for reform.

As the jury pool comes closer to being a true cross section of the community, it would seem inevitable that juries would in turn become more representative. Unfortunately, that is not always the case. The table shows, for example, that in San Francisco, nonwhites were 29.1 percent underrepresented on juries; what the table does not show is that, compared to the population, they were 17 percent *overrepresented* in the jury pool. In Atlanta, Camden, and in Delaware, too, nonwhites were much better represented in jury pools than they were on juries; in New Mexico, where *no* nonwhites served on juries, a significant number were included in the jury pool.

Just as you can attend a party and never be asked to dance, you can, as we have seen, be called for jury duty and never serve on a trial. And compared to whites, members of minority groups are not only far more likely to be challenged by an attorney, they are more likely to be excused by a judge.

Why would a judge "discriminate" in this way? The fact is that jury duty is more burdensome to some people than to others. Nowadays office workers and teachers—white collar workers, in general—usually continue to draw their regular salaries during the period of service. Workers in jobs that are paid by the day or the hour, however, do not. They are faced not only with the prospect of a loss of wages, but if they do not report to work daily, they may be in danger of losing their jobs. Jury service, then, becomes a serious threat to these people's very livelihoods, and, for this reason, they are likely to ask to be excused. Some judges have been known to grant exemptions automatically to those who can show that jury duty will be a severe economic hardship. Of course, if there is one group in which nonwhites and the young are likely to be substantially *overrepresented* it is among those for whom jury duty would be a serious financial sacrifice.

The solution to this problem is simple—and costly: require all employers to continue to pay the wages of employees on jury duty or require the states to raise jurors' pay to the level of a decent living wage. But in a time of galloping inflation, tight state budgets, and tax revolts, these solutions seem all but impossible.

In an interesting example of how the courts, apparently out of necessity, can make matters even worse, the New York State appellate court not long ago agreed that a suburban county may legally exclude from jury duty qualified citizens who do not have drivers' licenses. The ruling stems from the county's failure to provide adequate public transportation. If the only practical way to get to the courthouse is by car, it is self-evident that nondrivers must be excused. How much of that ideal cross section do *they* represent, anyway?

While the courts may keep juries free of the poor who don't own cars and laborers who dare not miss a day's work, their exemptions are as nothing compared to the weeding and pruning done by the lawyers. It should come as no surprise that the peremptory challenge is the single most powerful weapon for keeping members of racial minorities from sitting on juries.

Clarence Darrow, perhaps the greatest American defense attorney of the past century, once advised his colleagues to avoid affluent jurors "because, next to the Board of Trade, the wealthy consider the penetentiary to be the most important of all public buildings." In one of the Watergate-related trials, a social scientist, who, for a sizable fee, had been hired by the defense to assist in jury selection, recommended that "the college educated, Jews, and readers of the *New York Post* and *The New York Times*" be rejected. And as evidence for the prosecution we have the following excerpt from a training manual for district attorneys in the state of Texas:

WHAT TO LOOK FOR IN A JUROR.

A. *Attitudes*
1. You are not looking for a fair juror, but rather a strong, biased, and sometimes hypocritical individual who believes that Defendants are different from them in kind, rather than degree.
2. You are not looking for any member of a minority group which may subject him to oppression—they almost always empathize with the accused.
3. You are not looking for the free thinkers and flower children. . . .

Studies of case after case in which defendants are black show that prosecutors consistently use their peremptory challenges to eliminate blacks from juries. And defense attorneys do the same when they represent whites who are accused of criminally victimizing blacks. That black people figure significantly in the community is of no concern to attorneys during a *voir dire,* unless that fact can perhaps help them win the case. We cannot emphasize too often that defense and prosecution always muster all of their intelligence and skills in pursuit of a single goal—the acquittal or conviction of the defendant. Expecting either side or both to take pains to empanel a truly representative jury is like expecting the fox to protect the chickens.

Obviously, then, the chances that any group of jurors will comprise an accurate cross section of the community are not very good. One solution would be to eliminate peremptory challenges entirely. If all the answers given by a prospective juror during the *voir dire* prove acceptable to the judge—that is, if the judge finds no reason to dismiss the person for cause—that person must be empaneled. In 1974, such a bill was introduced in the Massachusetts House of Representatives. While it did not pass, some lawyers believe it is "an idea whose time is coming." Many more, however, are totally opposed to the end of the peremptory challenge, arguing that to deprive attorneys of this weapon is to limit the scope of the *voir dire* and thus the chance to uncover prejudicial attitudes in would-be jurors.

Well, then, critics reply, at least the number of peremptory challenges should be reduced. At present the number permitted to each side varies enormously from state to state—in capital crimes, for example, from a maximum of twenty-six, in California, to a minimum of four, in Virginia. Were attorneys allowed, say, only three to five peremptories, with the defense granted more than the prosecution, they would have much less power to distort the composition of the jury.

But what of those who find no fault with the status quo? For them, the adversary nature of a criminal trial provides all the protection a defendant needs. They are quick to concede that, when prosecuting a black, district attorneys often methodically reject as many of the blacks in the jury pool as they can. But, in turn, defense attorneys can eliminate the most bigoted whites. Both sides, then, remove those they consider the extremes. And if the jury that eventually results from this "exchange of fire" has a somewhat antiblack bias, the chances are that, however regrettable, this bias simply reflects the thinking in the community as a whole.

What effect does this have on a minority's chances of getting justice in our society? The obvious answer is that if members of racial minorities are kept out of the jury box and bigoted whites are admitted, those chances are substantially reduced. True enough, but as a means of forecasting jury performance in any one trial, that answer is about as dependable as an umbrella in a hurricane.

In Iowa recently, a male American Indian charged with murder faced a jury of eleven white women and one white man, while in New York City, not too long before, a black youth of sixteen accused of arson confronted a jury of nine white men and three white women, not one of whom was under forty-five. Both juries voted to acquit. Check the court records of any American city and you will find that such verdicts, although "unexpected," are not at all uncommon.

The point here is not that the underrepresentation of minorities on juries doesn't matter. It matters enormously. Time and again the Supreme Court has affirmed the right of a defendant to be tried by a jury composed of a true cross section of the community. We must continue to work to make that right a

reality: jury selection procedures must be made less discrimina-
tory and more democratic. But those who attack the jury system
because of its failings in this area overlook certain strengths
inherent in the system, strengths that significantly compensate
for the underrepresentation of one group or another. Why has
the Supreme Court refused to establish hard and fast rules for
minority group representation in jury pools? Because numbers
alone can neither promise nor prevent justice when it is people
who are being counted.

Controlling the Voir Dire

The fact is that efforts have been and are being made to restrict
the powers of the attorneys during the *voir dire.* Less extreme and
more successful than the Massachusetts attempt to kill the peremptory challenge, these measures may indeed lead to greater
minority representation on juries, but, we should quickly state,
that has not been their primary purpose. For the most part, they
have come in response to another major criticism of the jury
system—its inefficiency.

With enormous backlogs of criminal cases in so many legal
jurisdictions, courts search for ways to speed up the trial procedure, to "use up" fewer jurors—in short, to save time and
money. Surely one of the most effective ways to accomplish this
is by curtailing the *voir dire.* Thus, in fourteen states and in all
federal courts, attorneys do *not* necessarily enjoy the freewheel-
ing privilege of probing the beliefs and the very lives of prospective jurors.

There the *voir dire* is exclusively controlled by the presiding
judge, and he, at his discretion, may question prospective jurors
entirely on his own, allow the opposing attorneys to ask some

supplemental questions, or invite the attorneys to submit questions to him that he then may or may not choose to ask. The judge-conducted *voir dire* obviously serves to restrict the embarrassing and abusive interrogation that prospective jurors are so often subjected to. But it does significantly more: it saves precious time and, while it allows peremptory challenges, it inhibits an attorney from using the *voir dire* to create a sympathetic jury. A defendant, after all, has no right to a *favorable* jury, only to an *impartial* one, and a judge, with his experience and neutrality, should be best able to identify bias without tipping the scales to one side or the other.

Since in thirty-six states judges do not conduct the *voir dire,* we are safe in concluding that many (probably most) trial lawyers resist the idea vigorously. They maintain that in any one trial only the attorneys are truly sensitive to the particular prejudices that must be uncovered, and, therefore, only they can formulate the relevant questions that must be asked. Furthermore, they argue, the judge is a representative of the state, and by giving him total control of the *voir dire,* we are defeating the basic purpose of the jury system: protection of the rights of the individual from the oppression of government.

A compromise solution to this conflict, which has been adopted by several states, empowers the judge to ask the initial questions of each prospective juror and the attorneys to ask any follow-up questions they consider pertinent. The judge, however, retains the right to halt any line of questioning he deems inappropriate or offensive. Theoretically, at least, modified judicial control of the *voir dire* promises the court greater efficiency in jury selection, grants attorneys a fair chance to expose the unqualified, and protects prospective jurors from the worst excesses of questioning.

Excesses in the Jury Pool

Excesses of questioning are but one aspect of juror treatment that critics object to. There are other excesses as well, and they are all seen as evidence of the inefficiency of the system. What is particularly regrettable is that, in their effect, the excesses may seriously undermine our methods of achieving justice. For whenever the jury duty experience becomes a denial of such basic amenities as consideration and courtesy, the system falls short almost as badly as it does when it empanels a bigoted jury.

Indeed, the failings may in one respect be much the same: potential or actual jurors who are justifiably offended by the treatment they receive from the court and people who believe they have been excluded from the jury box because of race are likely to harbor similar feelings of resentment, hostility, and contempt. There is danger in such a reaction: the institutions that hold our society together can survive and flourish only so long as they retain the respect of the public they are intended to serve.

The first place to look for evidence of inefficiency and unconcern is in the jurors' waiting room, where hundreds of people sit staring into space.

We have already seen why the jury pool often contains more people than the courts are likely to need. But the fact remains that an excessive number of would-be jurors leads not only to wasted hours of waiting and the ultimate futility of having no opportunity to serve, but also to an avoidable drain on the public treasury—all those unnecessary people must, after all, be paid. To improve the situation, some communities have recently taken steps to coordinate the size and deployment of the jury pool with the reality of the courts' needs. For example:

—Several counties in New York State have set up a "phone-in system" which allows those on jury duty to call a central number every evening to find out whether they are needed the next day. If they are, they report and get paid; if they are not, they do not report and do not get paid.

—In a variation of the above, would-be jurors leave a number where they can be reached during the day. An hour before they are needed they receive a call, either at home or at work.

—Two of the smaller states are testing the "One Day or One Trial" experiment, in which persons not selected for a jury on the first day of service are automatically released. Of course, the next day another group of would-be jurors must appear.

—Night jury trials, in session from 5 to 11 P.M., have been established to reduce the backlog of felony cases and to make more efficient use of jurors and courtrooms.

—By expanding the master jury pool roster with names taken from supplementary lists, some courts have been able to cut the length of jury service from two weeks to one (unless, of course, a person is selected for a long trial during the initial five-day period).

—Some cities are actively promoting volunteer juror systems —encouraging people with leisure time to become part of the jury pool just by filling out a simple application. Increasing the size of the "volunteer army" obviously reduces the need for "draftees," but, of course, at the cost of representativeness.

The Fewer-Than-Twelve-Member Jury

Sometimes solutions to problems create problems of their own. The best-known method of reducing the demand for jurors—a method that, at least theoretically, saves the courts money not only by cutting down on the number of jurors needed but also by shortening jury selection and deliberation time—is also the oldest and most controversial: the fewer-than-twelve-member jury. In 1970, the United States Supreme Court upheld the constitutionality of six-member juries in certain criminal cases, declaring that twelve-member juries were a "historical accident" (one that dates, incidentally, to fourteenth-century England and probably does *not* derive from the fact that Jesus had twelve Apostles, as some have claimed). Before or since that time, thirty-eight states enacted legislation that permits smaller juries in civil actions while thirty-four have authorized them for some types of criminal trials.

Thirty-four states out of fifty certainly constitutes a trend (the holdouts, incidentally, are mostly in the Northeast), but is it a healthy one? Ironically, what jurors would probably consider the major advantage of the smaller jury is exactly what many legal scholars find so disturbing: it is easier for six people to reach agreement than it is for twelve. The critics argue that a speedy verdict is not necessarily the best verdict and the convenience of the jurors counts for very little when measured against the necessities of justice.

Recent surveys have suggested that the fewer the jurors the less likely they are to offer a fair cross section of community viewpoints, the less likely they are as a group to remember all the important pieces of evidence, the less likely they are to overcome their prejudices, and—because the possibility of a hung jury is directly proportional to jury size—the more likely they are to avoid deadlock and thereby convict an innocent person. In short, to quote the conclusion of one major study, twelve-member juries "produce longer deliberations, more communication, far better community representation, and possibly greater verdict reliability." For this reason the American Bar Association has recommended that a jury of twelve be required in criminal cases where the accused faces a penalty of six months imprisonment or more and another group of trial lawyers has adopted a resolution favoring twelve-member juries in *all* criminal cases.

Incidentally, eight years after declaring that six-member juries were constitutional, the Supreme Court ruled that five-member juries were not. While their decision was unanimous, the justices could not agree on a single overriding reason for it. One justice wrote, "The line between five- and six-member juries is difficult to justify, but a line has to be drawn somewhere if the substance of jury trial is to be preserved." The line, then, has been drawn at six, and, in spite of the critics, there it is likely to remain.

Nonunanimous Verdicts

If over the years the size of the jury has proved to be somewhat less than sacred, so too has the principle of the unanimous verdict. For jurors who suffer through countless agonizing hours trying to persuade a few holdouts to go along with the majority, the acceptability of a ten-to-two verdict, or a nine-to-three, would come as release from bondage. Some states have obliged them: in Oregon, for example, agreement by ten jurors out of twelve is sometimes enough for a verdict while in Louisiana only nine out of twelve is sufficient.

The purpose of such departures from tradition is, to quote the Louisiana law, to "facilitate, expedite, and reduce expense in the administration of justice." In the process, the states that allow majority (as opposed to unanimous) verdicts in certain criminal trials have eased the burden of jury duty considerably. But they have done so at a price: Here again critics charge a lack of verdict reliability. Just because decisions can be reached with reduced strain and conflict—just because the majority may at some point simply disregard the opinions of the minority rather than grapple with those opinions and try to refute them—less than unanimous verdicts are not the product of the full, robust, and intense debate that the jury system is intended to foster.

Videotaped Trials

Another certain way to "facilitate, expedite, and reduce expense in the administration of justice" would be to cut down somehow on the trial delays and the sudden and unexplained recesses that, with irritating frequency, shunt the jury from courtroom to jury room and back again and thereby cause increasing impatience. Considerations of juror displeasure aside, these interruptions are at the very least costly. Nevertheless, legal scholars would regard them as an essential if regrettable aspect of the jury system: as long as attorneys disagree about what is admissible evidence, who is a qualified witness, and which is the relevant statute, jurors, like misbehaving children, will continue to be kept out of the room. This, it is claimed, is the way it must be, particularly if the rights of the defendant are to be properly preserved.

But, surprisingly, someone has come up with an ingenious device that in effect eliminates the trial recesses that are so taxing for jurors and the state. An Ohio judge has pioneered the use of modern technology—specifically, the videotape and audiotape recorders—to produce an uninterrupted trial. In his courtroom, after the jurors have been chosen they are dismissed, free to go where they like, and the trial proceeds without them. From the attorneys' opening statements, through the taking of testimony (witnesses may even be questioned in a place outside the courtroom if that is more convenient for them), to the closing arguments, the tapes keep rolling, recording everything, and the jury box remains empty. Then, each side having rested its case, the judge assumes the job of a film editor, deleting all those pieces of tape that contain material he would have instructed the jurors to disregard had they seen and heard it. Everything that impeded the flow of the trial or that might improperly influence the jury winds up on the cutting-room floor. The jurors are then reassembled for the screening of a uniquely modern phenomenon, a "film" that has been edited by judicial ruling. The viewing over, the trial resumes and follows customary procedure: the judge's charge to the jury, the deliberations, the verdict.

In convenience, the benefits that videotape offers to a jury are too obvious to enumerate. But not only will the edited tapes be considerably shorter than were the actual proceedings—shorter and less distracting—from a judicial standpoint, they will be more conducive to a sound jury verdict. Because it presents to the jurors only what the judge believes pertinent, a videotaped trial produces, it is said, a more authentic kind of justice.

Not so, cry the detractors. Court proceedings, they argue, are more than the words spoken and the evidence exhibited. Even if there is some advantage in editing out what the judge considers objectionable, this is more than offset by the certain failure of videotape to capture the full atmosphere of a trial. What emotions did the defendant betray when various testimony was offered? How did his attorney look? At any one moment an alert and observant juror can take in far more than any camera can. And who will operate the camera, anyway? Not the judge surely, even though "editing" is at work merely in deciding what the camera will record, what it will ignore, and where it will be placed.

In a criminal trial, videotape probably creates more problems than it solves. It is certainly of no use when a trial is covered by the media and jurors sitting at home can learn from television and newspapers what they are not experiencing in person. Thus, while the videotaped trial is a worthy and interesting innovation, and one that has proved successful in civil cases, few criminal court jurors are likely to enjoy its advantages. They can expect to suffer through the delays and recesses just as they have always done.

Sequestration

Just as assuredly, on those infrequent occasions when trials are publicized, jurors can expect to be sequestered. But sequestration, too, has its critics and not only among those jurors who have been subjected to it. To begin with the obvious, it costs the state a lot of money (almost a quarter of a million dollars in New York City courts in 1978, with an additional $30,000 spent on transporting jurors to and from hotels). It can also pose logistical problems: not so long ago an acute shortage of New York City hotel rooms had court clerks calling suburban motels in a desperate search for beds for the weary. Said one clerk, "If I hadn't found rooms for them in a New Jersey motel sixty-eight miles from New York City, they would have had to sleep on the floor."

But sequestration causes concern on a deeper level as well. It may, critics say, produce precisely what it is designed to prevent: failure to view the evidence objectively.

If jurors can find no justification for being sequestered, which is often the case, they are inclined to be resentful of the state and, therefore, quite possibly, of the prosecution. If they object to being sequestered while the defendant is free on bail, their feelings may turn against the defense. And should their sequestration be prolonged, even more serious problems may emerge. For one thing, people who are able to leave behind their normal lives to serve for weeks or months on a jury are probably not truly representative of the community. For another, people who have spent a considerable amount of time together in virtual quarantine from the outside world cannot be said to be strangers to one another, as the law demands they be at the outset of the trial. The relationships they form may well have serious effects later on their deliberations. And finally, critics suggest, after a lengthy period of sequestration, jurors may simply not be the same people they were at the beginning of the trial. Who is to know what changes may occur in the personality of someone living for months in complete isolation from his or her normal existence? Who is to doubt that associating with a mere dozen or so people, all of whom have been exposed to exactly the same experiences, will rob a person of his individual perspective and the group of just those differences that the jury system is supposed to prize?

Can anything be done? In states where judges are required by law to sequester all juries once deliberations have started, attempts to relax the rule have run into powerful opposition from court officers. They contend that, because of juror exposure to outside influences, many more mistrials would result if deliberating juries were not sequestered, and thus a measure designed to save money would ultimately cost a great deal more.

A much louder uproar has greeted efforts to avoid trial-long sequestration. Since courts resort to the practice only when a case claims the attention of the press, judges have tried to solve the problem by banning reporters from courtrooms. Invariably, such rulings raise storms of protest. When the constitutional right to a fair trial clashes with the constitutional guarantee of freedom of the press, only the Supreme Court can resolve the conflict. While it has ruled that a judge may keep reporters out of a *pretrial* hearing in order to protect future jurors from possible exposure to the details of a case, in a 1980 decision it affirmed the right of the press to cover criminal trials. In the view of many, if sequestration is the price to be paid for press coverage of a trial, it is, after all, an inexpensive way to preserve the heart of the First Amendment.

*   *   *

These, then, are the principal complaints about the jury system from the critics who wish to uphold and strengthen it. We have seen how terribly complex are many of the issues raised by these critics. Almost every argument seems to spark an equally valid counter-argument, and almost every solution seems to leave new problems in its wake. As a result, jury reform is a gradual, lead-enly paced process, scarred by controversy and patched by compromise.

The Quality of Jury Performance

Standing apart from those critics who cry out for jury reform of one kind or another, there is that much smaller group that would respond, "Why bother? The situation is hopeless." With their attack directed at juror performance, these observers find most efforts at jury reform limited in value or of no value at all. For them, the use of the system itself must be severely restricted if not entirely abandoned.

"When a group of twelve men on seats a little higher than the spectators, but not quite so high as the judge, are casually observed, it may appear from their attitude that they are thinking only about the case going on before them. The truth is that for much of the time there are twelve wandering minds in that silent group, bodily present but mentally far away. Some of them are thinking of sadly neglected business affairs, others of happy or unhappy family matters, and, after the second or third day and especially after the second or third week, there is the garden, the house-painting, the new automobile, the prospective vacation, the girl who is soon to be married, and the hundred and one other things that come to the mind of one who is only partly interested in the tedious proceedings going on before him."

This commentary by a seasoned jury observer was written in 1937, but it could easily have been written today. Certainly if the ways of the jury system are slow to change, the ways of people are even slower. Consider the following, written almost forty years later, which characterizes a jury in a criminal trial as "a collection of persons of no special training or knowledge, no notable intellectuality, no particular awareness of the problems at issue, no strong ideology, no previous trial experience, and no clear ideas about the causes or control of crime. The principal qualification of the ideal juror is that he be an ignoramus about all the subjects to be discussed in the case at hand, and thoroughly underqualified to make expert judgments about the evidence he will be hearing."

This characterization may be a bit too scattershot in its attack: if nothing else, on any given jury there may be one or more persons who do have previous trial experience. But, of course, what is important in both these statements is not the accuracy of one observation or another but the common implication that ordinary people have no business deciding those grave questions of justice with which jurors are regularly confronted. They are too easily bored, says the first commentator; they do not have the background or the wisdom, says the second. A third might well accuse jurors of irresponsibility, since they have on occasion admitted that, totally bewildered by the conflicting evidence offered to them during the trial, they made their decisions solely on the basis of group pressure or, worse, by the mental equivalent of tossing a coin. And it would be all too easy to find a fourth critic who would charge that they are bundles of prejudice ready to burst at any time.

BALDWELL

To broaden and democratize the jury pool would do little to appease such critics. Indeed, opening jury service to nonvoters, for example, would if anything intensify their objections. And allowing fewer exemptions, excuses, and peremptory challenges would in no way "improve the quality" of the jurors chosen. Quite the contrary. If all the proposed reform measures in jury selection were to be implemented, they would simply fill jury boxes throughout the land with more of the "thoroughly under-qualified," more of the easily bored, more of the "ignoramuses" with short attention spans, and more of the bigots who disguise —or do not recognize—their bigotry. That such people are, after all, representative of the community is precisely the point: be-cause the very concept of the laymen jury springs from a belief that *all* citizens should have an equal opportunity to participate, the system is grossly inadequate as a means of achieving justice.

It is this argument that has caused some countries to abandon the jury system and others to refrain from instituting it. It is this argument that has led to the almost total disappearance of juries in civil trials in England and to their marked decline in civil trials in the United States. It is this argument that at least partially explains a rather startling statistic: nowadays, barely more than 10 percent of our criminal cases are tried before a jury. The great majority are settled by *plea bargaining,* a process that permits a defendant to confess to an offense less serious than the one with which he was originally charged in exchange for the promise of a lighter sentence. But many are tried by a judge alone.

Why should any defendant, while protesting his innocence, nevertheless choose to waive his constitutional right to a jury trial and put his fate in the hands of a single authoritarian figure? You can be sure that such a decision is not lightly made and usually reflects the informed judgment of a defense attorney. We have explained why lawyers on civil cases are inclined to avoid juries. If lawyers in criminal cases follow suit, often—though not always—it is because, given the nature of the defendant and/or the crime charged, they suspect that a reasonably impartial jury could never be empaneled. They will gladly risk wandering minds, even simple minds, but narrow minds could prove fatal.

To critics who challenge the idea of the jury system, no earthly precautions exist that would guard against bias within any group of six or nine or twelve people, however randomly or expertly they may have been chosen. And to find evidence of how devastating the power of bias can be inside the jury room, they simply turn the pages of our history.

It is a history studded with trials whose outcomes now seem infamous in their unfairness. When they occurred, they were perhaps branded as miscarriages of justice by a few or even a good many protestors. Today serious studies of these cases leave little doubt that their jurors acted on prejudice, often reflecting the prevailing political climate of the time, with little regard for the facts. To illustrate:

—In 1897, in a village near Hazelton, Pennsylvania, a crowd of mine workers—all Eastern European immigrants, most unable to speak English—marched in a demonstration to rouse their fellow miners to join them in a strike. A posse consisting of the local sheriff and his deputies fired into the group, killing nineteen of the marchers and seriously wounding thirty-nine. Tried by a jury of descendants of Yankee farmers, all Protestant, all Republicans, none mine workers, the sheriff and his deputies were acquitted of all charges.

—In 1914, a flamboyant Swedish-born union agitator named Joe Hill was found guilty by a jury of staunchly middle-class citizens of murdering a grocery store owner in Salt Lake City. The evidence against him seemed so flimsy that the Swedish Ambassador called for a new trial and the President of the United States twice asked that the verdict be reconsidered. But Joe Hill, later to be celebrated in song, was executed by a Utah firing squad in November, 1915.

—In 1920, two Italian anarchists, Nicola Sacco and Bartolomeo Vanzetti, were arrested on charges of having murdered a paymaster and a guard at a shoe factory in South Braintree, Massachusetts. They were convicted by a jury the following year, at a time when the difference between anarchy and Communism was clouded or ignored and people were alarmed into thinking that agents of the recent Russian Revolution were everywhere. Worldwide outrage greeted the jury's verdict and assailed the insubstantial evidence on which it had been based. For six years the day of ugly reckoning was postponed, but finally in August, 1927, Sacco and Vanzetti were electrocuted. Fifty years later, the Governor of Massachusetts "rehabilitated" them, declaring that prejudice had influenced the outcome of their trial.

—In March, 1931, a mob of whites dragged nine black youths

from a freight train, herding them to a jail in Scottsboro, Alabama, where they were charged with raping two white women. Early the next month, the "Scottsboro Boys" were tried by an all-white jury, convicted, and, except for the youngest, a thirteen-year-old, were sentenced to die in the electric chair. In November, 1932, their conviction was set aside by the United States Supreme Court, on the grounds that the defendants had not received adequate legal counsel; new trials were ordered. The following year two of the defendants were retried, again before all-white juries, and again both were convicted and sentenced to death, *even though in her testimony one of the supposed victims now denied that she or the other woman had been raped.* In 1935, the United States Supreme Court again reversed the convictions, this time ruling, historically, that the trials were invalid because blacks had been excluded from the panels of both the grand and petit juries. Later that year, a special grand jury, which, for the first time in Alabama since Reconstruction, included a black man, indicted the Scottsboro Boys for rape once again. In a series of trials held in 1936 and 1937, four of the original nine defendants were for the third time convicted of rape by all-white juries. (Rape charges were dropped against the remaining five, although one was convicted of assault on a deputy sheriff and sentenced to twenty years.) Their sentences ranged from seventy-five to ninety-nine years to electrocution, later commuted to life imprisonment by the Governor of Alabama, but over the next thirteen years all were paroled. In 1976, Alabama's Attorney General recommended a pardon for a defendant who was in violation of his parole, declaring that studies of the case indicated that this last of the Scottsboro Boys was innocent of the rape with which he had been charged forty-five years before. The pardon was granted by Governor George Wallace.

We like to believe that in the field of civil rights we have made "giant strides" since the 1930s, and it seems absurd indeed to think that, fifty years later, members of any minority group could suffer the agony that befell the Scottsboro Boys. Nevertheless, not so long ago a noted historian wrote, "One of the reasons that the United States Department of Justice has brought so few actions for criminal contempt of court by . . . voting registrars who have failed to heed court orders to register Negroes is that . . . juries will not convict these officials." Perhaps, then, today bias can acquit the guilty more easily than it can convict the innocent. But that bias can be the determining factor in any verdict robs the jury system of much of the moral force it was intended to have as a synthesizer of the voices of honorable people.

In Defense of the Jury System

Attacked and belittled, the jury system, with all its flaws, survives. How come? Simply because, like democracy in Winston Churchill's famous remark, it remains "the worst form . . . except for all those other forms that have been tried from time to time."

As we begin our defense of the jury system, let us consider what its severest critics would offer in its place: a single judge or a panel of legal experts—that is, X number of people well-trained in the law, presumably attorneys and/or judges. These alternatives to the laymen jury would, of course, enjoy the services of persons who are highly intelligent and eminently capable of keeping their attention fixed on the trial at hand and their prejudices tightly controlled. Like the judges and, increasingly, the panels of lawyers that hear and render verdicts in the great majority of civil suits, the criminal trial experts would be expected to have no trouble following the most complicated testimony, and, more important, they would recognize dishonesty in witnesses and deviousness in attorneys far better than jurors generally can.

What we have just described is an ideal. Let us now look at the reality: just how well are lawyers and judges likely to perform in determining guilt or innocence? To answer that question, let's look at how well they perform their present duties.

It is not our purpose to investigate or expose or even evaluate the legal profession, but having subjected jurors to all manner of stinging comment, it is only fair to note that none other than the Chief Justice of the United States has repeatedly commented on the "ineptness, the bungling, the malpractice which can be observed in courthouses all over the country." The rich and, much more frequently, the poor complain about the quality of the legal services available to them. There are, of course, thousands of thoroughly qualified attorneys—capable, hardworking, ethical men and women—in practice today. But there are thousands of others who—whether they be rated by seasoned courtroom spectators, judges, jurors, law school professors, or their own clients —would get considerably less than passing grades.

As for the judges, they, too, have in recent years been the target of heavy criticism. Not so long ago a national magazine featured on its cover the small head of a judge timidly emerging from a mountainous judicial robe, one many sizes too large for the perplexed-looking man inside it. The illustration embodied the message: many judges cannot fill the job they have been entrusted to do. Whether appointed or elected, judges are all too frequently seen as political hacks who have attained their seats on the bench not by their knowledge or accomplishments but by staying in the good graces of political party chieftains. In some of the more common complaints, judges are accused of being arrogant, corrupt, lazy, incompetent to the point of senility, and

—an old friend—bigoted. (We should note, for example, that in the little chamber of jury-trial horrors we just visited, all the guilty verdicts were upheld on appeal by judges who chose not to recognize the bias on which those verdicts were based.)

Again, the obvious truth is that there are superb judges serving in courtrooms everywhere—people not only of great legal experience but also of wisdom, understanding, compassion, discipline, patience, fairness, and total integrity. Whether rare or common in a government of laws not men, it is these exemplary guardians of justice who make the laws work.

But, in the eyes of many of us, apparently, the laws do not work well enough. In a 1978 poll of the population in general and of judges, lawyers, and community leaders in particular, public confidence in state and local courts ranked below that of the medical profession, police, business, and public schools. Can anyone question that it is the judges and the lawyers who must bear the major responsibility for this absence of trust?

If, then, lawyers and judges are, on the whole, performing their present roles rather less than impressively, surely it is misguided to thrust upon them the additional function of the laymen jury. But the case against the suggested alternatives to the jury system goes considerably deeper than that. For the sake of argument, let's assume that only the most dedicated and able men and women of the law, of the highest judicial caliber, were called on to replace juries in our criminal trials. What happens then is not something we can only imagine, for the fact is that all fifty states permit a defendant, except in the most extraordinary circumstances, to waive his right to a jury trial and appear before a judge alone, a procedure known as a *bench trial.* At least a third of the men and women tried for major crimes do put their trust in the judge. But statistical analysis shows that the more serious the crime charged, the more likely the accused is to opt for a jury trial. One study shows jury waivers in 70 percent of drug violation cases, 50 percent of forgery cases, 32 percent of robbery cases, and only 13 percent of murder cases. That same study indicates that defendants or, more realistically, their lawyers have good reason for choosing as they do: the more serious the crime, the more likely a jury is to acquit.

Other studies have shown quite consistently that in jury trials the judge agrees with the jury's verdict about 75 percent of the time. In a tiny percentage of the cases, judges are inclined to acquit while the jury convicts. *But in about 20 percent of the cases, juries are more lenient than judges would have been.* Either they acquitted when the judges would have convicted, or they convicted on a lesser charge than the judges would have. In that finding, the difference between the jury system and its suggested alternatives stands revealed.

There are several broad areas that breed disagreement between judge and jury. Among them are:

—The judge knows certain facts relating to the case—for example, a defendant's previous criminal record or a confession that he made but later repudiated—that by law must be kept from the jury.

—Judge and jury view the evidence differently—most often this translates into their believing or disbelieving the testimony of one or more witnesses.

—Judge and jury view the defendant differently—which usually, although not always, means that the jurors feel greater sympathy for him.

—Judge and jury view the law differently, with the judge sworn to uphold it and the jurors ready to ignore it, either because they believe it to be a bad law in general or because they feel it should not be applied in a particular case.

Where these differences in thinking between judge and jury

exist—and, remember, they exist to a significant extent in no more than one case in five—they are not the product of chance or accident. The judge is a figure of authority, trained in the law, experienced in dealing with crime and criminals. It is to be *expected* that he will see people, events, and laws differently from ordinary citizens. Indeed, it was in reaction to this very fact that the jury system came into being. As a symbol of democracy, it was intended to bring the perspectives of ordinary citizens to questions of justice. If our government is, as Lincoln said, "of the people, by the people, and for the people," the people should be able to decide if one of their number has violated a law of the state. The judge alone is too good for this task and therefore not good enough. Because he is of high social and economic standing, he may not accurately reflect the prevailing values of the community. Because he has been so often exposed to lawbreakers, he may let his knowledge of the past cloud his perception of the present. Because he is deeply schooled in the law, he may consider it more precious than freedom is to the rest of us. Because he is a figure of authority, he may not identify with the ordinary man who stands before him.

Thus, it is the "ordinariness" of the jury that finally emerges as its unique strength. What sets the jury system apart from all other methods of determining guilt or innocence is that ideally it alone allows a person to be judged by others just like him— people who come from the same community and share its values, people who have had similar experiences, people who have been tempted and have not always resisted, people who feel remorse for what they have done and perhaps regret for what they have not done, people who know how thin the line between guilt and innocence sometimes is. If juries are more inclined to be lenient than judges, it is because in any randomly selected group of twelve or even six, there may be a few men and women who will think and say much sooner than any judge could:

"From the time he was born that guy's life has been one bad break after another."

"My husband deserted me and I had to raise two kids all by myself. I know what it's like when you can't give them a Christmas present."

"Okay, so they broke into the building and burned the records. What were the records for, anyway? To send eighteen-year-olds over to die in a country no one ever heard of."

"I believe her because I know sometimes you feel so alone and so tired and battered that you don't want to fight anymore. You'll confess to anything just to be left in peace. But that doesn't mean what you're confessing is true."

"I read in the paper a few months ago about a man who served eight years and then somebody else confessed to the crime. In those eight years he never saw his son. He wouldn't let his wife bring him to visit because he didn't want the kid ever to be inside a prison. When the man got out, the son was ten years old. He missed all that lovely growing up, and y'know why—because of eyewitnesses."

"When my father came to this country he didn't speak a word of English, and, of course, he couldn't read it. The one time he got arrested it was because he couldn't understand what a sign said. When I think of that gentle, bewildered man being hauled into a police station, I want to laugh and cry at the same time. So don't tell me that ignorance of the law is no excuse. Sometimes it is."

"I've lived long enough to know that nothing ever happens without a reason and sometimes—not always, but sometimes—the reason makes all the difference. A man who steals to eat shouldn't be treated like a man who steals to buy himself a Mercedes. I'm not saying the first man shouldn't be punished, but more often than not, it seems to me he gets punished a lot worse than the second man. And it should be just the opposite."

Jurors who make comments like these probably know little about law books and legal precedents. But without instruction they are doing exactly what the law wants them to do. Juries, in reaching their verdicts—verdicts they are commanded to pronounce but never to justify—are expected to draw upon their own humanity, upon what they have learned by living. If this makes them more compassionate, more willing to forgive, more accepting of error, and more inclined to doubt than a judge—whose every decision requires explanation—would be, the benefit to the defendant is precisely what our legal system would have him enjoy. For even with the presumption of innocence, a defendant is no more than one person against the state, and the odds he faces are great. Juries bring those odds just a bit more into balance.

*   *   *

The jury system in America today is sadly imperfect. It is in need of all kinds of reform and improvement. Yet most of the time it works. Although a noted turn-of-the-century philosopher described a jury as "twelve people of average ignorance," survey after survey has shown that however their minds may wander, most jurors remember what must be remembered; however unsophisticated their backgrounds, most jurors understand fully the case at hand—the evidence, the indictment, the law. And if jurors are not as successful in overcoming their biases, even in this regard they surely perform better than a society still deeply scarred by discrimination has any right or reason to expect.

For jurors in criminal cases are usually better than the rest of us; paradoxically, they are better than themselves. When they step into a jury box, they feel challenged as they have probably never been before. They know so much depends on them that they try as hard as they can to apply their intelligence and their common sense and their learning to the task at hand. They never forget who or what they value, but at the same time they recognize that other people may be the same or different without being any less deserving of justice.

We are being too idealistic, no doubt. Not all jurors rise to such heights. Some remain mired in their prejudices and therefore blind to the facts. But enough do not to allow a system that begins with ordinary people, chooses among them in the most haphazard and frequently unfair way, and treats the chosen with minimal courtesy and concern—to allow such a system to achieve compassionate justice with impressive regularity. It is exhilarating to be part of such a system. True, jury duty can often be a burdensome ordeal, but just as often it can be a stimulating challenge, a chance to take part in a real-life drama, and an occasion to learn about other people—and yourself. A summons to serve may sometimes prove to be a ticket to two weeks of boredom, but just as often it can be a passport into a world you will enter as a stranger and leave as an honored citizen.

Bibliography

Bonsignore, John J., et al., eds. *Before the Law: An Introduction to the Legal Process.* 2nd ed. Boston: Houghton Mifflin Company, 1979.

Gross, Kenneth. *The Alice Crimmins Case.* New York: Alfred A. Knopf, 1975.

Hunt, Morton. *The Mugging.* New York: Atheneum, 1972.

Kalven, Jr., Harry, and Zeisel, Hans. *The American Jury.* Chicago: The University of Chicago Press, 1966.

Kennebeck, Edwin. *Juror Number Four: The Trial of Thirteen Black Panthers as Seen from the Jury Box.* New York: W. W. Norton & Co., 1973.

Lincoln, Victoria. *A Private Disgrace: Lizzie Borden by Daylight.* New York: G. P. Putnam's Sons, 1967.

Litwack, Leon F. *Been in the Storm So Long: The Aftermath of Slavery.* New York: Alfred A. Knopf, 1979.

Morris, Richard. *Fair Trial: Fourteen Who Stood Accused from Anne Hutchinson to Alger Hiss.* Rev. ed. New York: Harper Torchbooks, 1967.

Norris, Clarence, and Washington, Sybil. P. *The Last of the Scottsboro Boys.* New York: Putnam, 1979.

Novak, Michael. *The Guns of Lattimer: The True Story of a Massacre and a Trial, August 1897–March 1898.* New York: Basic Books, 1978.

Phillips, Steven. *No Heroes, No Villains: The Story of a Murder Trial.* New York: Random House, 1977.

Rembar, Charles. *The Law of the Land: The Evolution of our Legal System.* New York: Simon & Schuster, 1980.

Simon, Rita James. *The Jury and the Defense of Insanity.* Boston: Little, Brown and Company, 1967.

Starr, Isidore. *The American Judicial System.* New York: Oxford Book Company, 1972.

"Judging the Judges." *Time,* August 20, 1979.

Timothy, Mary. *Jury Woman.* Palo Alto, Calif.: Emty Press, 1974.

Van Dyke, Jon. *Jury Selection Procedures: Our Uncertain Commitment to Representative Panels.* Cambridge, Mass.: Ballinger Publishing Company, 1977.

Villasenor, Victor. *Jury: The People vs. Juan Corona.* Boston: Little, Brown and Company, 1977.

Zeisel, Hans, and Diamond, Shari Seidman. "The Effect of Peremptory Challenges on Jury and Verdict: An Experiment in Federal District Court." *Stanford Law Review* 30, no. 3 (1978): pages 491–531.

Zerman, Melvyn Bernard. *Call the Final Witness: The People v. Darrell R. Mathes as Seen by the Eleventh Juror.* New York: Harper & Row, 1977.

Index

I am deeply indebted to Shari Seidman Diamond, Assistant Professor of Criminal Justice and Psychology, University of Illinois at Chicago, and to Leroy B. Kellam, Judge of the Criminal Court, City of New York. Their assistance and advice were of inestimable value.

I am grateful also to all those—too numerous to cite—who recalled for me their experiences as jurors, to my family for their help whenever it was needed and their forbearance throughout the writing of this book, to Pat Allen for her belief in the project, and especially to my editor, Marilyn Kriney, for her patience, judgment, and skill.

Melvyn Bernard Zerman
September, 1980

347.73
Zer

Zerman, Melvyn Bernard
Beyond a reasonable doubt:
inside the American Jury ...

347.73
Zer

Zerman, Melvyn Bernard
Beyond a reasonable
doubt: inside the Ameri-
can Jury System

DATE DUE	BORROWER'S NAME	

MEDIALOG
Alexandria, Ky 41001